LOCAL DEVELOPMENT PRACTICES AND INSTRUMENTS IN WEST AFRICA

AND THEIR LINKS WITH THE MILLENNIUM DEVELOPMENT GOALS

A SYNTHESIS OF CASE STUDIES FROM UNCDF PROGRAMMES IN:
BENIN, BURKINA FASO, GUINEA, MALI, NIGER AND SENEGAL

UNCDF

UNITED NATIONS CAPITAL DEVELOPMENT FUND

United Nations Capital Development Fund
Two United Nations Plaza, 26th Floor
New York, NY USA 10017
Site web: http: / / www.uncdf.org

UN Sales No.: E.08.III.B.7
ISBN: 978-92-1-126215-5

The projects which are the subject of the present capitalization would never have come into existence without the technical and financial partners of UNCDF, in particular UNDP, FBS, the Grand Duchy of Luxembourg and the European Union, to which we express our sincere gratitude.

The following have contributed to the drafting of this document:
Coordination of the study:
  • Christian FOURNIER, Regional Technical Advisor, West Africa, UNCDF
Drafting of the synthesis of the six (6) countries:
  • Simon-Narcisse TOMETY, Consultant
Drafting of capitalization reports by country:
  • Aime GNIMADI, Consultant, Benin
  • Oula Claude OUATTARA, Consultant, Burkina Faso
  • Mamadou Lamine BAH, Consultant, Guinea
  • Hamidou ONGOIBA, Consultant, Mali
  • Saidou HLIDOU, Consultant, Niger
  • Papa Babacar DIOUF, Consultant, Senegal
Participation in the review of the synthesis document:
  • Boubacar FALL, UNCDF Programme Officer, Senegal
  • Djoume SYLLA, UNCDF Programme Officer, Mali
  • Henry GLOURIEUX, UNCDF Programme Officer, Niger
  • Blaise TCHABI, UNCDF Programme Director, Benin
  • Oumar WADE, PADMIR Coordinator, Senegal

Photos and design: Adam ROGERS / UNCDF

TABLE OF CONTENTS

List of acronyms

ADECOI	Project in support of Communal Development and Local Initiative in Bourgou
AFD	French Development Agency
AFVP	French Association of Volunteers for Progress
AIP	Annual Investment Programme
ANICT	National Investment Agency for Local Authorities
APRC	Association of Presidents of Regional Councils
BSF	Belgian Survival Fund
CAD	Committee for Analysis of Dossiers
CCC	Communal Council Centre
CDD	Committee for Dialogue on Decentralization
CDP	Communal Development Plan
CFIAS	Community Financial and Institutional Analysis System
CMC	Commune Management Commission
DCDC	Departmental Council for Dialogue and Coordination
DGF	Decentralization Grant Fund
EIG	Economic Interest Group
ESCDP	Economic, Social and Cultural Development Programme
GCO	Grassroots Community Organizations
HDI	Human Development Index
IGA	Income-generating activities
IVLUC	Inter-village Land Use Commission
LACF	Local Authority Capital Fund
LAIF	Local Authority Investment Fund
LDC	Least Developed Country
LDF	Local Development Fund
LDF	Local Dialogue Framework
LDP	Local Development Plan
LDPG	Local Development Programme in Guinea
LDSP	Local Development Support Programme
LOC	Local Orientation Committee
MDG	Millennium Development Goals

MEF	Ministry of the Economy and Finance
MIP	Multi-year investment programme
NCU	National Coordination Unit
NGO	Non-governmental organization
NOC	National Orientation Committee
NOLA	National Office for Local Authorities
NRIP	National Rural Infrastructure Programme
NRM	Natural Resources Management
OTPA	Office of the Treasury and Public Accounting
PACR/TM	Support project for the rural communes of Timbuctu and Mopti
PADEL	Local Development Support Project in East Borgou and West Atacora
PAPNA	Namentenga Province Agro-pastoral resources development project
PD	Participatory diagnostic
PRS	Poverty Reduction Strategy
PRSP	Poverty Reduction Strategy Paper
RCP	Rural Council President
RDA	Regional Development Agency
RDP	Rural Development Project
RDSP	Rural Decentralization Support Programme
RFP	Request for proposal
ROC	Regional Orientation Committee
SBP	Sahel Burkinabe Programme
SBP-SP	Sahel Burkinabe Programme Support Project
SFAC	Steering and Funds Allocation Committee
SPFS	Special Programme for Food Security
UALE	Union of Local Elected Officials
UNCDF	United Nations Capital Development Fund
UNDP	United Nations Development Programme
UNOPS	United Nations Office for Project Services
VDC	Village Development Committee
VLUC	Village Land Use Committee
WFP	World Food Programme

FOREWORD

It is a pleasure and an honour for me to present this report on UNCDF's contributions to local development and decentralization in West Africa. This report represents a synthesis of studies on UNCDF work in six countries of the sub-region (Benin, Burkina Faso, Guinea, Niger, Mali and Senegal). Its purpose is to present efficient thinking and approaches to local development and also to stimulate and support an exchange of ideas among practitioners, locally-elected officials, citizens and development partners.

We do not pretend to have produced an exhaustive study of the problems and dynamics of decentralization and local development in West Africa. Rather, we wish to move the discussion in such a way as to advance decentralization and local development policies and encourage policy makers and practitioners to take the Millennium Development Goals (MDGs) into account in all activities at the local level.

This study fills an important gap pertaining to the weak visibility of decentralization and local development in West Africa along with the lack of knowledge surrounding the community development experiences in rural areas. This region of Africa is a constantly evolving testing ground for experimentation. New approaches and tools are tried while others are improved; so that governments and development partners can make use of them in the achievement of the MDGs. It is in this context that we are pleased to present our experiences and to show how governments, local authorities and citizens can work together as a team to solve the problems they are facing.

This report presents an analysis of the political and legal contexts in which local development projects take place and explains how this environment influences their implementation. It also highlights the difficulties UNCDF and its development partners face in implementing decentralization policies and programmes in the region. Furthermore, the report describes the instruments and tools commonly used in UNCDF's decentralization and local development projects and focuses on the development results obtained. Finally, the report pays a great deal of attention to partnership in all its forms. On a broader note, the report seeks to link decentralization and local development in local communities in rural areas with the achievement of the MDGs.

We believe this study fills an important gap among practitioners worldwide concerning decentralization and local development in West Africa. It also makes a valuable and unique contribution to knowledge about community development experiences in rural areas. This region of Africa is a constantly evolving testing ground for experimentation. New approaches and tools are tried while others are improved so that governments and development partners can make use of them to help achieve the MDGs. It is in this context that we are pleased to present our experiences and to show how governments, local authorities and citizens can work together to solve the problems they are facing.

I would like to express my appreciation to our UNCDF colleagues in the countries concerned, our development partners and collaborators and to our closest and most important partner, the UN Development Programme, with whom we worked closely in every country and without whom this study would not have been possible. Lastly, I would like to express my special and deep appreciation to Christian Fournier, UNCDF's Regional Technical Advisor in West Africa, who was the leader and driving force behind this important study.

Richard Weingarten
Executive Secretary, UNCDF
September 2007

EXECUTIVE SUMMARY

The mission of the United Nations Capital Development Fund (UNCDF) is to reduce poverty and strengthen local governance in the least developed countries (LDCs), due to the breadth and depth of their poverty. The Human Development Index (HDI) (2005) shows a very low ranking of the six countries covered in this report, which are among the poorest in the world: Senegal (157), Guinea (160), Benin (161), Mali (174), Burkina Faso (175), and Niger (176). The strategy developed by UNCDF to reduce poverty in the LDCs is based on two mechanisms: inclusive finance and local development programmes.

The documented experiences of the projects co-financed by UNCDF in the six countries of West Africa concern pilot projects in support of decentralization and local development, particularly in rural areas. They are included in national poverty reduction strategies, which result from the international commitments of these countries, and refer to the Millennium Development Goals (MDGs). The following lessons have emerged from the descriptive and analytical synthesis developed in this document:

1. Institutional context and political-administrative architecture

The texts composing the legal framework for decentralization and local development in the sub-region are rooted in national constitutions, resolutions from national conferences, and programme statements (as in Guinea). All the Constitutions have established the principle of free administration of local authorities by elected councils and affirm that these communities constitute the institutional framework for exercising local democracy. This principle was reaffirmed in the legal arsenal specific to decentralization in these countries.

The institutional architecture of local government organization shows three levels of deconcentration for Senegal, Burkina Faso, Guinea, Mali and Niger, and one for Benin. It includes four levels of decentralization for Senegal, three for Mali and Niger, two for Burkina Faso and Guinea, and one for Benin.

Local and regional elections in these countries are mainly controlled by political parties; the leadership of local public life is strongly influenced by the political class in power, which becomes a monopoly of one class to the detriment of others. Different consultative forum for dialogue have been established, however, to foster dialogue among various local actors. Also, with few exceptions, such as Mali, candidacies independent of political parties are authorized in local and even national elections.

The powers that have been transferred to local authorities are those considered important for combating poverty and promoting local development. They include the civil registrar, the administrative police, the management of local development projects, land use planning (bidding for public services in water, health, education, etc.), environmental protection and sustainable management of natural resources. Also included are coordination of investments and development activities, promotion of local economic development, inter-community affairs and decentralized cooperation. In Senegal, however, some essential administrative powers such as the productive sectors (agriculture, livestock farming, fisheries, etc.), rural water supply, sanitation and transport, have not yet been transferred to local authorities.

Decentralization has given rise to many fears and questions among the local populations. Today, interest in its expansion can be observed everywhere. While the competences transferred are justified by the failure of state centralism and difficult living conditions of the communities, on the other hand, the political will to support implementation of decentralization should be more strongly represented in order to reverse the trends of the past. Indeed, a legal framework and a variety of instruments to make decentralization concrete are certainly essential but not sufficient to promote sustainable local development. This reflects an inadequate phasing of interventions by different public and private actors within the framework of a coherent policy linking decentralization and deconcentration. In this regard, the transfer of resources is not going smoothly in all the countries concerned, but the long-term perspectives are optimistic.

2. Intervention areas

The geographic characteristics of the intervention areas are as follows: (i) they are very far from the capitals (up to 1,500 km in the case of N'guigmi in Niger); (ii) they are located in areas with low rainfall or right next to the Sahel and subject to recurring ecological and food crises; and (iii) they have a very high agricultural potential but are isolated and not considered for improvement, such as in Benin and Guinea.

All the projects are involved in decentralization and support local authorities and local organizations.

It can be observed from examining the overall features and issues below that choices of intervention areas were determined by their advanced degree of poverty: (i) famine and malnutrition; (ii) monetary poverty; (iii) the production base in rural areas relying on depleted natural resources; (iv) adult illiteracy and low schooling rates of children; (v) difficulty in accessing drinking water and health care; (vi) low level of socio-collective investments, poor hygienic conditions, and deplorable conditions for improving living standards; and (vii) lack of institutional and organizational capacity to promote local development.

These characteristics of the intervention areas show the importance of decentralization in allocating responsibility to local actors for managing local affairs. In particular, they demonstrate the value of land use planning to allow each local government to become a part of the country's development process, irrespective of its geographical situation. Ultimately, decentralization offers new possibilities for reducing inequalities in access to basic collective services among the different regions of a country and allows the specific conditions of each area to be taken into account on the basis of national solidarity.

3. Main tools

The local planning exercise produced three documents in the UNCDF partner communes:

- the *communal development plan* (CDP), which is a long-term guidance and framework tool covering a period of five to six years;
- the *multi-year investment programme* (MIP), which operationalizes the CDP by programming the investment needs and investment resources to be mobilized over the next three years;
- the *annual investment plan* (AIP), which serves as a budget programme for the year and allows for the implementation of the CDP from a results-based approach. This approach leads an annual evaluation of communal performance to assess the performance level of local development objectives.

These local planning documents are prepared in a participatory manner. The MIP is supported by the Local Development Fund (LDF).

The financial mechanism is based on the LDF and is included in a budget support scheme to local governments. Communal project management and the principle of budget support ensure that all bidding process and contracting procedures take place at the commune level. In contrast to conventional interventions where work, equipment delivery and services provision are centralized in the project management unit, here each commune carries out the procedures for realizing its investments. In countries where the communes are not yet active, the inter-village land use commissions (IVLUCs) exercise their powers with the limitation of not being legally authorized to mobilize local resources through taxation.

Eligibility for the LDF leads to the determination of financial allocation to communes, evaluation of the performance of the communes at the end of each year, the principle of budget support to strengthen traceability, transparency and co-financing. In addition to these intervention procedures, the UNCDF expert advisory mechanism, which was made up of the project team and the service providers, have allowed for better structuring of services expected by partner communities. In particular, a toolbox is created for each project to: (i) develop planning and budgeting instruments; (ii) formulate, propose and protect micro-projects; (iii) develop expertise in the management procedures for the various LDF counters; and (iv) manage facilities.

The LDF is a financial tool that offers many distinct qualities: (i) integration into the public finance circuit of each country to familiarize the communes with financial and accounting procedures required by the laws on decentralization; (ii) a lever effect on the financing system; (iii) mobilization of local financial resources; and (iv) a multi-purpose tool focusing on social-community services, the local economy, natural resource management (NRM), food security, a reduction women's burdens, and capacity-building of actors (public and private) involved in local development.

The implementation of a system of planning and promotion of local governance and LDF has had the following impacts: *at the social level* (participation of marginalized groups and impoverished communities in the decision-making process, access to community services); *at the financial and economic level* (professional formation of local workers, creation of income-generating activities (IGAs), increased tax and non-tax revenues in the commune); *at the environmental level*, through reforestation activities, soil protection and restoration; and *at the land use level* through an fair distribution of investments on the basis of objective and agreed criteria (educational and health maps and networks of water points), limiting the influence of favouritism or political-partisan clientelism.

Nevertheless, it should be pointed out that due to the inadequate level of many locally elected officials and agents of local governments, these various tools have yet to be fully utilized. The progress made is still due to major reliance on the expertise of advisory groups and project structures. This situation is understandable considering that very few communes have qualified technical services. Most communes are just getting started and assistance will be necessary for several years to come. The duration of the planning process needs to be highlighted, which often represents a constraint in project start-up for the populations concerned.

4. MDGs

The approaches to assistance used by the UNCDF projects have led to the promotion of an open process that includes the poor and marginalized groups, and that allows the interests of all actors involved and all social strata to be taken into account in local planning.

The organization of the communes and the composition of the established structures transcend all traditional divisions (social and, particularly, political membership; place of residence, etc.) and take into account the interests of the various groups involved, irrespective of their power relations. This inclusive process occasionally corrects the lack of representation on communal councils observed in most countries.

Finally, the nature and functionality of the investments realized are indicators of the voice of the poor because they show that the needs of local populations have been taken into consideration. These voices are what help prevent the failure of development projects. The achievement of the MDGs depends on the active role and responsibility of the poor in the decision-making process in general, and in the development of their community in particular.

In light of the above, the UNCDF projects distinguish between different levels of investment: (i) investments at the local level of general community interest and/or specific to an organization working on a particular activity; (ii) investments on a supracommunity scale, between the village and the commune; and (iii) investments to strengthen institutional capacities of communal institutions, involving the town council offices and their intermediaries only.

Although it has been well established that the records on UNCDF project achievement are fully in line with the MDGs, it should be emphasized that the internal monitoring and evaluation system for these projects and the communes themselves is not yet linked with the MDGs as far as reference indicators are concerned. It would be useful to conduct a reference study on partner communes concerning MDG criteria and indicators in order to follow their evolution. When such a system becomes operational at the commune level, the MDGs would need to be brought to the local level to strengthen the monitoring of planning tools, even for projects that began before the MDGs.

5. Partnership

In the implementation of support programmes for decentralized local development in West Africa, UNCDF and its project teams develop partnerships at the local, national and international levels. UNCDF believes partnership is more than a necessity; it is a fundamental choice in the poverty reduction strategy to achieve the MDGs.

These partnerships take several forms: institutional, operational, formal and informal. They have given UNCDF projects leverage in investment financing, knowledge sharing and joint initiatives.

UNCDF experience has shown that marginalization of local representatives of decentralized state services in the implementation of projects creates frustration and blockages in the field. At the same time, the procedures for involving these technical services are rarely explicit in the project formulation documents. Only flexibility in the financial structure of this component allows for the use of expertise that can be mobilized among this category of actors. But the underlying problem is found in the weakness of national deconcentration policies, especially at the budget level, which prevents the decentralized state structures from operating optimally.

INTRODUCTION

This document examines a group of projects implemented by UNCDF in West Africa over the past ten years in Benin, Burkina Faso, Guinea, Mali, Niger and Senegal, made possible, among other factors, through financial partnerships with other development partners.[1] It presents a synthesis of six studies on these countries. The objective of this synthesis is to present lessons learned from UNCDF experiences in local development in West Africa, in part through its support to decentralization, and to understand the conditions that must be set in order to obtain significant results and impact in development and to improve the overall living standard for the people in the intervention areas.

This synthesis allows: (i) to exchange and disseminate UNCDF knowledge on best practices; (ii) to better understand the institutional and social blockages that can limit the approaches tested; (iii) to understand how these pilot projects were able to affect the achievement of the Millennium Development Goals (MDGs).

Therefore, analysis of the case studies per country allowed for documenting the lessons learned, obstacles and innovations related to different pilot experiences.

Their synthesis follows this format:

- Presentation of the institutional context and the political and administrative architecture of the UNCDF-financed projects.

- Presentation of the intervention areas, the elements justifying the choice of these areas, and the intervention goals.

- Discussion of the various tools and approaches tested on support to decentralization and local development, drawing on general and specific lessons learned regarding tools and procedures, methods of operation and innovations.

---

[1] Luxembourg, the Belgian Survival Fund, UNDP, the European Union, the governments of countries cited, the local authorities in project areas and finally, the local populations of these authorities.

- Highlighting how the project approaches and measures concretely help to achieve the MDGs, with regard to ensuring that the voices of the poor and disadvantaged are heard regarding their choices of investments; the framework used to measure impacts and effects; and the adjustments to be made to systems and models of local planning in order to integrate the MDGs.

- Highlighting the reasons motivating UNCDF to automatically call for collaboration of several partners for UNCDF-initiated projects and how this partnership takes shape, by characterizing its different forms according to its results, the steps followed to its conclusion, methods to ensure its success, and the risks and pitfalls to be avoided.

The methodological approach for this synthesis is essentially based on documentation from the six basic reports produced in the countries mentioned above. The individual studies are available in French on UNCDF's website at www.uncdf.org.

For each chapter, the approach consisted in: (i) gathering and synthesizing the relevant thematic information contained in the six reports to highlight the essential common characteristics and the specificities in the data regarding the context, instruments and approaches, links with the MDGs and partnerships; (ii) conducting a thematic and comparative analysis according to the success/failure/potential/opportunities (SFPO) method.

Tools have also been created and formatted based on the instruments and analyses described in the country reports. These tools provide access for users to detailed descriptions and modus operandi of the instruments and approaches that gave good results.

Also, a synthesis of the lessons learned was produced to conclude each central theme of the report.

The only difficulty encountered was a lack of harmonized statistical data or their absence for certain sub-topics, which did not permit equal treatment of data. In such cases, it was decided to illustrate certain case studies or provide ranges.

Finally, the structure of the document is also in line with the plan above.

1] CONTEXT AND INSTITUTIONAL FRAMEWORK FOR DECENTRALIZATION AND LOCAL DEVELOPMENT

1.1. General context of the sub-region

The history of decentralization in West Africa dates back to the colonial period, with the set-up of local governments from some towns from each of the six countries. But the political regimes that followed in these countries since their accession to national sovereignty have not always favoured the consolidation, unity and generalization of local authorities. Nevertheless, all the political regimes in these countries have always spoken favourably of participatory management of the country and closer ties between the civil service and the population. This vision often took shape either through promotion of local advisory bodies operating as forums for collaboration and social dialogue or through promotion of community development programmes and projects focused on giving responsibility to local communities.

In most of these countries, the 1960s to the 1980s were marked by revolutionary, military or socialist regimes that were more or less centralized, led by state parties and partisan public administrations. The institutional failure of these States, which were characterized by, *inter alia*, their ill-advised debt, the spread of poverty and their inability to address the problems of development, led to the establishment of structural adjustment programmes (SAPs) to comply with the World Bank and the International Monetary Fund. These programmes were intended to reduce state spending, launch modernization, and reduce civil service staff, liberalize the economy and reform public finance. In addition to these institutional characteristics common to the sub-region, countries of the Sahel such as Niger, Mali and Burkina Faso also faced chronic food crises, which continue to affect their economies, particularly the living conditions of the disadvantaged communities in towns and the countryside.

The 1990s marked a decisive political turning point on the path towards democratization for these six countries as a whole, in particular, towards the transfer of political power. Three elements or factors form the basis of this decentralization process.

The first factor relates to openness to democracy, to a certain extent coming from pressure from the local populations, but also from development partners. These partners have increasingly placed conditions on their assistance in pursuit of greater democratization. This may also be understood as a spreading of democracy at several levels, from the local to the central.

The second factor that drove decentralization was related to the crisis of state public finances. States no longer having had the capacity to manage centrally and had to find new ways to manage and deliver public services. Decentralization, by the transfer of authority, could provide an appropriate response to this pursuit of greater efficiency and effectiveness in public service.

Finally, the third factor is urbanization: Africa is urbanizing or "municipalizing", and this dynamic is not going to stop. Consequently, local authorities will become an even greater demographic and economic burden in the future. A response must therefore be found to the emergence of the local entity as the appropriate place for this new arising democracy, as well as for the provision of public services according to the principle of subsidiarity. The other significant aspect was to ensure territorial balance and to give both rural and urban authorities the means to offer substantial public services and to become catalysts for development in general.

These factors contributed to an acceleration and expansion of preliminary approaches to decentralization, by incorporating lessons learned from land use programmes tested at the village or inter-village level. Consequently, rural areas will not be marginalized from considerations of democratization, decentralization and urbanization. Many experiments based on research and action were implemented throughout Africa, in particular, in West Africa. In this context, village development councils or committees (VDCs) were democratically elected by the population to manage community affairs. Their roles are assisted by technical commissions or working groups, which help to extend the area of strategic analysis of the situation, mobilize the local populations and circulate information. According to the country, the VDCs had legal status covered by an administrative act or were considered a project implementation means without further institutional formalities, but nevertheless have statutes, local natural resources management codes, and settlement dispute rules.

Following the example of certain technical and financial cooperations (UNICEF, World Bank, German Cooperation), these community-type structures have also been supported from 1995 to 2002 by UNCDF projects in countries where the State has not yet created communal structures. While significant progress could be made in motivating local communities through the village planning process and by allocating responsibility to villages for managing their common interests, it is also true that the level of spatial analysis at the villages is limited to their community. There is not enough coherence, therefore, with a land use planning approach that requires work and coordination at various territorial levels with the aim of promoting harmonious and sustainable local development. Once decentralization comes into effect in a country, the entry point for local development for UNCDF projects is therefore no longer the community approach, but rather the communal institution, through local project management. The commune thus becomes a major decision-making centre for local development, the combat against poverty, resource mobilization and the sustainability of collective services for the populations through its annual investment budget.

The community approach of the UNCDF projects is a transitional arrangement allowing to establish and manage community infrastructure in the sectors of village water supply, basic education, health, (the village health unit), rural roads, and natural resources regulation and protection. Legally, the public ownership of this infrastructure and its recurring costs comes under local public works. Socially, VDCs have promoted a relational dynamic, which had often allowed for real intermingling of the various interest groups that make up the local governments. Furthermore, the Venn diagram tool, widely used in community development methods, clearly identifies the categories of actors, their relationships and power relations involved so as to implement a community development approach that integrates, rather than distances, certain categories of groups.

It is clear that this approach escaped the influence of numerous political parties in the election of community leaders making up the VDCs. The VDCs were able to set up veritable field training schools in participatory democracy and community leadership development, having improved the relationships between community leaders and other categories of institutional actors (representatives of the civil service, development partners), for protecting the public interest and maintaining basic social control. It must be acknowledged, however, that this model has also given rise to some inconsistencies due to the proliferation of committees within a single community and the lack of integration of medium-term development plans.

Today, the community-type approach is practised by some donors. This causes many difficulties in effective setting up of sustainable local governments when some donors marginalize them and adopt a community approach, denying these structures created from decentralization policies.

In sum, the major issues in decentralization and local development in the UNCDF countries of intervention are the improvement of the living conditions in disadvantaged communities in towns and rural areas by offering social and community services that are available, accessible and sustainable.

To achieve this, it is essential that the development process assign responsibility to local actors, both in identifying their own needs and in carrying out activities to meet them. In this way, the civil service and programmes supported by external partners may facilitate and concretize appropriate solutions for communal project management.

In light of the above, most countries have drawn up decentralized rural development policy letters with the goal of linking the competences of local governments with the community development approach and sectoral public policy. This policy emphasizes:

- strengthening the technical and management capacity of the rural population, local governments and their basic structures so that they may better respond to priority needs in essential social and economic infrastructure;

- establishing short-term mechanisms to directly transfer to local governments the financial resources necessary for their development, and, in the longer term, establishing mechanisms allowing them to mobilize those resources themselves;

- establishing operational frameworks for dialogue, decision-making and monitoring and evaluation, involving all actors in decentralized rural development;

- setting up tools for land management for securitization of investments;

- establishing participatory mechanisms for increased transparency in local development management.

If the relevance of the choice of governments for a gradual transfer in the decentralization process is recognized, this transfer must also have visibility according to a realistic and predictable time scales or time chat. In this way, the local populations may better understand the political will to transfer authority and resources to local authorities. This also assumes that decentralization goes together with deconcentration, so that state services responsible for supervising local authorities and providing them with necessary consultation are prepared to play their role efficiently and effectively. Many implementation texts on decentralization laws have not yet entered into force and in certain cases, not all the levels of decentralization have yet been set up. Although there is a basic legal framework to allow gradual decentralization, despite missing clarifying regulations, there are serious problems with lack of coherence between sectoral public policy and community policies advocated by the states through decentralization. This means that centralism remains strong in administrative culture and that the political will to transfer the powers of national public resources management to local authorities remains weak.

Finally, an effort to raise awareness and provide information is needed to ensure a better understanding of decentralization by state agents. Their understanding of the issues involved in this state reorganization is key to the success of community policies, especially local development programmes. The principle of subsidiarity must therefore pervade the directions and approaches of various levels of government in order to improve programmes' efficiency and effectiveness to combat poverty and enhance their positive impact on the daily lives of vulnerable groups.

1.2. Legal framework of decentralization and local development

The goal of decentralization is to ensure the harmonious development of all local authorities on the basis of national solidarity and regional and local potential in order to combat poverty. The texts making up the legal framework for decentralization and local development in the sub-region are rooted in national constitutions, resolutions of national conferences and programme statements (as in Guinea).

The link between decentralization and local development

The legal framework in the six countries shows that decentralization is inconceivable without local development. As part of a process of local administration reform, decentralization creates a dynamic environment for the expression of local democracy and allows the exercise of power at the local level. It should: (i) facilitate citizen participation in managing local public property through its decentralization element; (ii) establish connections between the citizen and the administration; (iii) lead to citizens taking responsibility for their own affairs; and (iv) help promote the economic potential of local governments through the exercise of decision-making power by the local populations at the local level through their elected representatives.

The legal framework (laws, ordinances and application decrees) of decentralization establishes decentralized local authorities, and gives them legal personality and financial autonomy. The Constitutions of all six countries under study have stipulated the principle of free administration of these local authorities by elected councils, and affirm that local governments constitute the institutional framework for exercising of grassroots democracy. This principle was reaffirmed in the legal arsenal specific to decentralization in these countries.

In addition, the legal instruments have defined the jurisdictions of the local authorities, the common property, conditions of eligibility for local councillors, management bodies and their functioning, budget structure and funding sources, areas of competence of the local authorities, and supervisory prerogatives, as well as the mechanisms, allowing the local populations to exercise social control over the management of these authorities.

Each local authority has an assembly whose denomination and composition depends on the number of levels of decentralization and the titles of the administrative districts. In countries with many levels of decentralization, a distinction is made between the regional council, the council of the area or department, and the communal council. According to the country (Senegal and Guinea for example), rural communes are given the title of "rural community" or "rural development community". All these councils are deliberating bodies whose members are locally elected officials. They are responsible for defining local public policy in their respective local districts in compliance with the laws of the Republic and the national development guidelines, and monitoring their implementation.

At the level of local governments, the mayor (executive body of the commune) or the president of the rural community is the top official of the community, and accordingly, is the head of communal administration. At the regional level, this position is occupied by the president of the regional council. However, there is no hierarchical relationship among the various deliberating bodies. The separation of powers among them is based on the principle of subsidiarity. On the other hand, the mission of the region is to promote an operational linkage among the various levels of local authorities for coherent and harmonious development of the region. For example, in Senegal, this mission of integration is facilitated by the *Agence régionale de développement* (ARD, Regional Development Agency) and *Plan de Développement Régional Intégré* (PDRI, Integrated Regional Development Plan), two instruments managed by all the authorities on the basis of their respective competence.

1.3. Administrative organization of States and local authorities

1.3.1. Local organization

The organization of local administration is practically identical in the subregion as a whole, with the exception of Benin. The institutional architecture of local government organization shows three levels of deconcentration for Senegal, Burkina Faso, Guinea, Mali and Niger, and one for Benin. It includes four levels of decentralization for Senegal, three for Mali and Niger, two for Burkina Faso and Guinea, and one for Benin. These are levels where the central authority (supervisory body) and a range of decentralized state services (technical expertise, and implementation of public sectoral policies) are represented. With the exception of Benin, all the countries have begun regionalization, or at least have a legal framework instituting it. In Senegal and Mali, regionalization is truly operational with regional assemblies that deliberate on local policies for which they are responsible. However, territorial divisions at the same level do not have the same title in these countries. A department in Senegal corresponds to a province in Burkina Faso, a *cercle* in Mali and a prefecture in Guinea, while the name "department" in Burkina Faso refers to an arrondissement in Senegal, a commune in Mali and a sub-prefecture in Guinea. In contrast, a department in Benin represents the only level of decentralization and is not comparable to a region, but first-level administrative constituencies where the communes are under supervision.

At the level of local authorities, the juxtaposition of decentralization and deconcentration predominates. This co-territoriality is complete in Mali. It is partial in Senegal, Burkina Faso, and Niger, where local authorities share two levels of territorial division with administrative constituencies, as opposed to three. However, in Guinea, the sub-prefecture in the rural development community does not have jurisdiction over this community; this prerogative belongs to the prefecture. Co-territoriality is totally absent from the institutional architecture of Benin: the department (territorial district) and the commune (local government) are not at the same territorial level.

Table 1: The institutional architecture of decentralization

Country	Territorial division	Number and type of local authority	Synthesis of territorial system
Benin	*Départment* (12)	Commune (77)	One (1) level of deconcentration One (1) level of decentralization
Burkina Faso	Region (13), province (45), *départmem* (350)	Region (13), commune (351), i.e. 49 urban communes and 302 rural communes	Three (3) levels of deconcentration Two (2) levels of decentralization
Guinea	Region (4), prefecture (7), sub-prefecture	Commune (422): urban commune and rural development community	Three (3) levels of deconcentration One (1) level of decentralization
Mali	Region (8), *cercle* (49), commune	Region (8), *cercle* (49), commune (703)	Three (3) levels of deconcentration Three (3) levels of decentralization
Niger	Region (11), *départment* (34), *arrondissement*	Region (8), *départment* (36), commune (265)	Three (3) levels of deconcentration Three (3) levels of decentralization
Senegal	Region (11), *départments* (34), *arrondissement* (103), villages	Region (11) and communes (387) including 67 urban communes, 43 communes of the *arrondissement* and 320 rural communities	Three (3) levels of deconcentration Two (2) levels of decentralization

The architecture of territorial divisions set out in table 1 is based on heterogeneous sizes of local authorities. In total, there are 2,205 communes in the six countries, 87 per cent of which are rural.

Mali, where communal boundaries were established on the basis of the free choice of villages and subdivisions that wished to merge, has the most communes in the sub-region, with a total of 703, of which 523 have under 17,000 inhabitants. This number represents the average population of a Malian commune. An estimated 15.1 per cent of Malian communes have under 5,000 inhabitants; 15.6 per cent have over 20,000 people. This disparity affects the economic viability of communes that greatly depend on the population's ability to contribute.

In Senegal and Burkina Faso, on the other hand, a commune must have a population of at least 10,000, compared with 5,000 in Benin and Guinea. However, the demographic size is highly variable and uneven, both within each country and between countries. The average population of a commune is 70,000 in Senegal, 35,000 in Burkina Faso, and 39,000 in Niger. These figures should be viewed with some scepticism, however, because they include the national capitals, which automatically creates an imbalance and significantly inflates the average. In reality, if the large communes are removed from the calculations, only small communes remain.

If the average surface area of communes in Mali is 1,700 km^2, that of the commune of Salam in the Timbuktu region is 1.22 times the entire surface area of Benin and 0.7 times that of Senegal. In Niger, there is some contrast between communes, with areas varying between 500 km^2 on average in the south to over 10,000 km^2 in the far north. The rural commune of N'Gourty, an UNCDF commune of intervention in Niger, covers 96,000 km^2, with a widely dispersed population of 23,000 spread over 265 villages. From the point of view of land use management, it is difficult to share infrastructure among communities, such as schools, health centres, and village water supply pipes due to the distances separating most of the villages. Moreover, the lack of a critical mass required by users of community social services poses problems in investment optimization and returns. The cost of combating poverty in these vast, isolated and sparsely-populated areas is thus higher than elsewhere for the same needs. These areas require greater solidarity at the national level to avoid marginalizing the populations concerned.

1.3.2. Representativeness of local authorities

In all six countries, the basic laws or codes for the local authorities have stipulated elections to designate representatives of the populations on the deliberating bodies for all local authorities. The number of elected members of the deliberating bodies is also regulated by law and adjusted according to the population of each electoral district, and therefore the local authority as a whole.

There are more than nine communal councillors in all countries, with a maximum of 49 per local authority. For those countries that have provided for a deliberating body at the regional level, their composition is variable, between 52 and 62 members in Senegal, 15 to 41 in Niger, and 7 to 31 in Guinea. The size of communal and regional councils in each country generates an impressive number of locally elected officials. For example, there are more than 13,000 elected officials in Senegal, around 18,000 in Burkina Faso and 1,199 in Benin. This obviously poses a major problem for any capacity-building programme given that the great majority of these elected officials are illiterate and cannot use written material, and thus do not benefit appropriately from training programmes.

Generally, communal, municipal and regional councillors are elected by universal suffrage for a five-year term, except in Guinea where the term of office is four years. Voting at the regional level includes a quota of representatives from each department within the regional council (in Senegal).

Political affiliation, other than for the election of the President of the Republic, is required when running for elective office. Local and regional elections are highly controlled by political parties and local public leadership becomes the monopoly of one class over another. On this point, Senegal has chosen not to accept independent candidacies for local and legislative elections, which therefore excludes a major part of the electorate from the management of local affairs. This situation is no better in the other countries (Benin, Guinea, Mali, Burkina Faso, Niger), which have opened up these elections to independent candidates. The six countries end up with the same politico-partisan configuration of the deliberating bodies of local authorities.

While an overstaffed communal council is difficult to manage and costly to maintain, it is unacceptable that such a body cannot be representative of the majority of the local community. On the other hand, in Mali, the electoral system does not take into consideration territorial representation of local communities (villages, sections and neighbourhoods) within the communal council. Thus, of the 11,160 local communities in the country during the 1999-2004 mandate, 65.58 per cent did not have a member on a communal council; for the current term (2004–2009), the percentage rose to 66.20 per cent. Consequently, some influential villages or subdivisions dominate local political life and make up the heads of political party lists at elections. This situation cannot be criticized from a legal standpoint, but will have consequences for citizen involvement in the life of their community. Certain villages justify not paying taxes by having no elected official from their community on the communal council. What is important is not that each village have its elected representative on the council, but that there is local representation, at least for a group of neighbouring villages. Benin has been successful with local representation, not by ensuring one representative per village, but by preserving the old administrative districts, the *arrondissements*. Each *arrondissement* is represented by two elected officials on the council.

The risks of recentralizing local power

In most of the countries and in many local governments, there is a type of recentralization of power towards the influential local village communities because of their prior history and their demographic weight. The larger a country, with its population widely dispersed over its territory, the greater the tendency for local power to be seized by those who hold traditional and religious power in the locality. This holds true in Mali and Niger, in particular.

The representiveness of local councils is a delicate and complex issue that cannot be ignored because it is fundamental in a decentralization process whose raison d'être is local participatory democracy, where local citizens are actively engaged in resolving their problems themselves. Above all, it involves making the local government a common project of its inhabitants. Also, a local election is important not only for bestowing legitimacy, but as an integral part of the social identity each local authority. Each local community therefore wishes to recognize itself through its elected councillors, who together form a local mini-parliament. This is the reason that the role of local civil society must be supported and strengthened.

**Maintaining strong ties between the commune
and each of its administrative units**

Widely dispersed housing—which should be resolved in decentralization through appropriate administrative supervision of the population and its increased participation in management of local affairs—is a disadvantage where local governments are too vast and thinly populated. To address this, Burkina Faso has added a village level to the institutional pyramid of decentralization in the form of village development committees (VDCs). Taken from the model of the village land use committee (VLUC), together they represent the rural community of a department.

These VDCs have development plans, which are linked with the rural community development plan, and are authorized to manage the development tasks in the village area. A decentralized national programme for rural development goes together with responsibility for tendering and contracting process of local investments. This community strategy for structuring rural communes is based on: a demands-driven support approach for village communities; a support approach through flexible funds to finance the priorities of the VDCs; a economic development approach based on cooperation, synergy and coherence; and a modular approach to adapt financial tools according to the various levels of the institutional structure of the decentralization.

The village is not a level of decentralization in Burkina Faso and Senegal; it has no legal status but can have financial autonomy in certain cases. This approach is also in effect in Benin with the national development programme conducted by the communities (NDPCC). Yet unlike in Burkina Faso, communities benefiting from this programme are responsible for managing community projects, for which there are legal provisions. This rural communization based on the land use management approach results from experiences developed in this field by the World Bank and UNCDF. UNCDF and many donors, including the French Development Agency (AFD) argue in favour of true ownership of tendering and contracting process by the commune, and it is then up to the commune to decide if it will commit itself to project management for the benefit of the local communities by delegating management authority. UNCDF does not favour this type of community approach when there are local authorities existing legally within the framework of decentralization laws. It therefore promotes an approach that respects national political commitments through decentralization laws that recognize the commune as having rights and responsibilities for tendering and contracting process.

1.4. Evolution of the decentralization process

Locally elected officials everywhere have inherited a command administration with an institutional profile showing an inability to collaborate with civil society organizations, usually incapable of integrating modern local management techniques, and above all, difficulty in adapting to decentralization. In a related manner, the degree of autonomy provided by law is hindered by the weak technical and financial ability of staff and locally elected officials, which explains the strong dependence on the state and its services.

1.4.1. Competences transferred

In the six countries, the competences (powers and responsibilities) of the state and local governments are defined and distributed by the legislature on the basis of a certain number of principles:

- **Gradual transfer** (training, gradual acquisition of independent means of operation and investment, appropriation by results-based management capacity and taking into account the complexity of the dimensions of competence);

- **Subsidiarity** (a relevant anchor for powers and responsibilities);
- **Proximity** (users' accessibility to local public services);
- **Concomitance** (any transfer of competence from the State to the community is accompanied by a concomitant transfer of resources to enable them to manage their new responsibilities).

According to the sector and political will, the distribution of competences among local authorities takes into account the way each public utilities and services sector is organized. It therefore takes into account the health pyramid (community health centres, area health centres, regional hospital centres), the various levels of the education system (pre-school, primary, general secondary, high school, vocational training), and the direction of local and regional development priorities established by the country.

As a whole, the competences of local authorities concern:

- management of the civil registry and archives;
- civil protection, assistance and emergency aid;
- carrying out of local and regional development plans so that each local authority develops its potential, exploits opportunities, and resolves problems that arise in the community through the production models and consumption systems that characterize it;
- promotion of economic, educational, social, health, cultural and scientific development in the region, the commune and the rural community;
- land management, real estate management and urban planning;
- environmental protection and natural resource management;
- coordination of development investments and activities for harmonious, balanced and sustainable development of local authorities, taking into account the interests of different social groups (the majority, minority, privileged and disadvantaged, local and non-local partners) of the nation as a whole;
- promotion of smooth exchanges between the various levels of local authorities for coherent and harmonious development of the region for consolidating national unity.

Each local government enjoys its own full decision-making authority in terms of its juridical personality and financial autonomy. In sum, the principle of free administration is established for each level of decentralization, even in countries where there are several levels of local authorities, such as Senegal, Mali, Niger, Guinea and Burkina Faso. There is no hierarchy of local authorities, therefore, but functional relationships. In general, transfers of competence have suffered from a lack of transfer of resources in the countries of the sub-region. Moreover, the transfer technique adopted favours the "sharing of competences" and the lack of block transfers of competences in the name of the principle of gradual transfer.

1.4.2. Local governments and their management capacity

The communal council (or municipal for communes with special status, or rural council for rural communities), the cercle council, and the regional council represent the assemblies elected by the populations to manage the affairs of the commune, *cercle* or region. The administration of these various bodies is coordinated by general or community secretaries, whose skills level depends on whether the commune's budget allows for recruiting staff with the required qualifications. Generally, they are state agents or the local authority made available or subsidized by the state budget.

As the deliberating body of the local authorities, these different councils have decision-making authority that they exercise by deliberations in legally specified matters, notably, the budget, the development plan of their local jurisdiction, the overall outline for land use and urban planning, economic, social, health, scientific, sports and cultural development, environmental protection, enhancement of living standards, inter-communal cooperation and decentralized cooperation.

The mayors' roles and responsibilities go far beyond those assigned to the local structures that preceded them. In Benin, for instance, the administrative position held by the mayor corresponds to that of the sub-prefect before decentralization. These sub-prefects were generally senior officials (civil administration, taxation, social affairs or labour). Alternatively, they were from various categories of middle management (educators, agricultural agents, security officers), and did not therefore necessarily have the required background for these posts.

In Benin, the only educational requirement approved by law to be eligible to become mayor is the knowledge of reading and writing. Yet the country has only one decentralization level and a small number of communes (77), with a limited number of elected posts (1,199 elected officials). Communal elections attract intellectuals, either the youth without schooling, retired or outposted civil servants, or relatively educated entrepreneurs.

In Mali, mayors have replaced heads of *arrondissements*, and the level required is middle management (equivalent of the *baccalaureat*). Malian law allows elected officials in general to be illiterate, from the President of the Republic down to local officials, including deputies to the National Assembly and heads of deliberating bodies. As in Mali, in Senegal an impressive number of presidents of rural councils and their deputies are illiterate because

the requirement "to know how to read and write" included in the local cooperation framework (LCF) in the country is not implemented. In all countries
without exception, there is a problem in reaching a balance between democracy
founded on legitimacy and on the confidence of the electorate, and the basic
skills of locally elected officials regarding their mission in all the countries.

In order to maintain a team dynamic within these deliberating bodies
and harness the expertise of resource persons, the legislature has prescribed
required committees and the possibility for each local authority to set up
additional committees (permanent or temporary) to study and monitor issues
referred to it. In general, the three required committees encountered in all the
countries of the sub-region are: (i) the economic and financial affairs committee; (ii) the land use and environment committee; and (iii) the social and
cultural affairs committee.

In order to broaden these areas for consultation and proposals, all legislation has prescribed cooperation, coordination and coherence frameworks,
with varying titles but virtually the same missions and objectives.

Places of power and struggles for influence
in the conquest of local power

While local powers are exercised at the local authority level through regional,
municipal or communal councils and rural councils, it has been established in
many countries that the influence of traditional and religious leaders remain
significant in social control and popular expression, especially in rural areas.
Indeed, traditional leadership still exerts a strong influence in the social and
political arena. Although these leaders have no particular jurisdiction in relation to local authorities' competence, they are at the heart of the electoral system, irrespective of level considered. All elections, whether national, regional
or local, presidential, parliamentary or municipal, have always demonstrated
the important and inescapable reality of the traditional, influential chiefdoms
(historical legitimacy) in the conquest of institutional state power. This is a
requirement for the political system in order to mobilize the electorate.

Indeed, at the institutional level and downwards to create local government at the commune level, decentralization is placed on a terrain that is not
uncharted. These areas were already centres of power (authoritarian power of
governors, prefects, sub-prefects representing the state, but also the traditional
power of tribal chiefs). It is also an intervention framework for the decentralized state services and projects, as well as an open terrain for other types of
activities conducted by new independent actors—associations, national and
international NGOs, and many rural organizations spontaneously established
by the local populations or created under various development programmes
and projects—that the communal management bodies cannot leave out.

In other words, communalization is now part of a landscape already structured by traditional powers, the decentralized state services (state representatives, technical services), which are by now accustomed to relations of authority. Sometimes long and well-established local development actors (communities, associations, NGOs, projects, etc.) are also present in this landscape, who are more experienced and possibly have more means than the local authorities.

Regional and departmental authorities, although planned and organized on a legal and territorial level, still have far to go in terms of their functionality and visibility (Senegal, Mali), and are not yet operational in Niger and Guinea.

1.4.3. Supervisory authority

According to the level of decentralization and deconcentration, supervisory authority is entrusted to the governor of a region or the prefect of a province, department or district.

The exercise of the supervisory authority includes three main functions: (i) assistance and advice to local authorities, the support of their actions and their harmonization with the actions and policy directions of the State; (ii) monitoring of the legality of actions taken by the communal council or mayor, the regional council and its president; and (iii) budgetary control, which should be strictly exercised by means of approval, cancellation or substitution. Governors and prefects are supported in their mission by cooperation and coordination frameworks, whose composition varies according to the country but whose basic motivation remains identical: improving the circulation of information and acting in synergy.

Actions of communes subject to approval by the supervisory authority generally involve:

- mode of management of communal property;
- travel abroad by the mayor and his deputies;
- individual decisions on appointments, promotions and penalties submitted to the disciplinary council for review, and the dismissal of commune staff;
- the communal budget and its amendments during the budget period;
- procedures for implementing local taxes, fees and tariffs, and setting tariffs and other non-tax resources, as well as collection methods;
- the amount, guarantee period and method of reimbursement for advances and loans;
- naming of public streets, squares and buildings;

- preparation of all urban planning documents;
- agreements concerning public markets and local concessions for industrial or commercial public services.

All the countries have access to a dialogue mechanism on local public policy. Two models synthesize the various inclusive advisory group mechanisms and cooperation frameworks found in the sub-region. It is useful to distinguish the Benin and Senegalese models. In all the countries, decentralized structures depend on these cooperation frameworks; they are barely or not at all operational due to lack of resources, but also due to significant differences between the line of authority of the Ministry of the Interior, under which Governors and prefects depend, and the head offices of sectoral ministries represented locally, who depend on their central ministry.

In the Benin model, there are two dialogue frameworks provided by law:

***Conférence administrative départementale* (CAD, The Departmental Administrative Conference),** the mechanism for state advice and counsel, presided over by the prefect of the department, and includes directors and heads of departmental services only. This technical framework, which is a type of departmental council of ministry representatives, aims at coordinating government action in each department.

***Conseil départemental de concertation et de coordination* (CDCC, The Departmental Council for Dialogue and Coordination),** presided over by the prefect of the department, includes the mayors and their deputies, a representative from the departmental union of rural producers, a representative of the departmental consular chamber, and a representative of the departmental federation of school parents. This obligatory consultative body on economic, social and cultural development programmes in the communes and on their coherence with national programmes is the main framework for formalizing relationships between the State, the local authorities and civil society in each department. The CDCC makes recommendations on the following only: (i) the land use management plan and development projects within the department; (ii) environmental protection measures; (iii) proposals to merge, separate and change the boundaries of the departmental authority or of communes composing it, and (iv) disputes arbitration between communes. Finally, no director of a decentralized state technical service sits on the CDCC; the prefect represents them.

In the Senegalese model, there are three levels of dialogue framework, but each integrates the *State/central government* (supervisory authorities, decentralized services), *local authorities and civil society.*

Commission régionale de développement **(CRD, The Regional Development Commission),** which is presided over by the governor assisted by two deputies (administration, development), includes the various local authorities of the region, the representatives of decentralized state services, civil society and other structures. This consultative body for coordinating development activities, in contrast to the Benin model, merges the CAD and CDCC. In sum, the CRD is more integrated with actors. The same configuration can be found in the *Comité départemental de développement* (CDD, Departmental Development Committee and the *Comité local de développement* (CLD, Local Development Committee). However, the dialogue frameworks mentioned for Senegal (CRD, CDD and CLD) no longer have a legal basis since Act No. 96-06 came into effect.

An assessment of the exercise of supervisory authority shows much confusion among all members of chain of jurisdiction: government, governors, prefects and local authorities. In many cases, the agents of state authority (governors and prefects) continue to treat communal and municipal authorities as if they had some kind of hierarchical power over them. Some locally elected officials, from mayors to councillors, continue to be submissive on their own to the prefects by not affirming the independence of the administration that the law provides the local authorities. This situation can be explained by a limited understanding of the laws. At the same time, other locally elected officials have difficulty accepting the role of prefects in their communes or pretend to be unaware of it, thereby giving the impression that they only wish to accept supervision when it suits them; this leads to greater conflicts of institutional leadership.

Conflicts occasionally arise between the governor or prefect and the local authorities over competition for use of the local representatives of decentralized state services that are under the administrative supervision of the governor and at the same time make up the technical committee of the regional development agency headed by the regional president (as in Senegal). Regional or departmental services have a strong tendency to lean towards the orientations determined by the national directorates on which they depend in terms of budget allocations, advancements and transfers, to the detriment of operations in the region and the local commune.

In addition, attempts by political parties to control appointments to the office of governor and prefect in certain countries are one of the reasons behind the mistrust of directors and heads of decentralized state services for these senior state representatives of territorial administrations. This lack of consistency between decentralization (devolution to local government) and "deconcentration of central government" (state devolution) is the result of a regionalization without a real policy behind it, which weakens the power of state authority agents in the regions or departments over the local representatives of decentralized state services.

1.4.4. Advisory approaches

Although the name varies from one country to another, each has a ministry in charge for decentralization. In Benin, Niger and Guinea, decentralization co-exists with public security, while in Senegal, Mali and Burkina Faso, a ministry deals specifically with territorial administration and local governments.

Each country also has a expert advisory structure to serve the local governments—such as the *Maison des élus locaux* (House of Elected Officials) in Senegal, the *Maison des collectivités locales* (the Local Authorities Office) in Benin or the Association des Maires de Burkina Faso (MABF, Mayors' Association of Burkina Faso)—with missions of training and capacity-building, decentralized cooperation and institutional support. These structures are still weak, however, and often still have a tradition of not sharing information with all their members.

Technical expert advisory services of the State for the benefit of local authorities are also weak, even in countries where the legal frameworks have specified the procedures for making them available. The underlying problem is still the institutional weakness that has worsened over the past two decades with recruitment freezes, ageing of staff, lack of budgetary resources, corruption and politicization of appointments, which do not necessarily allow recognizing competent people.

If Mali's decision to privatize support and advisory services seems justified in this regard, the Malian model is based on a concept of projects benefiting from support from various development partners. The essential question is whether Malian communes, especially rural ones, will be able to bear the cost of such expertise in the medium term. Similarly, will private service providers adjust their costs according to the communes' capacity when they know that the viability of many communes is uncertain? Further, will the State be able to make additional efforts to support partnership between communes and private providers of support and advisory services?

All these questions show that decentralization *is not a simple administrative and territorial reform: it is a time-consuming process of state re-organization that requires experimentation with many approaches to find the solutions to the problems encountered.*

In each country, local authorities are also interlinked by one or two national associations of elected officials according to the number of decentralization levels, which include national and regional associations of communes or mayors, national associations of rural councils, and associations of rural council presidents. An umbrella organization brings together all these associations of local authorities in Senegal, i.e. the Union of Associations of Local Elected Officials (UAEA). All these associations of elected representatives provide a space for solidarity, advocacy and lobbying.

Missions of the regional development agencies (ARDs) in Senegal

These missions include: (i) coordination and harmonization of investment plans and programmes of action between the State, the region, on the regional scale, and among the various local governments; (ii) implementation of land use, environmental and sectoral plans at the regional level; (iii) drafting and monitoring of agreements making external state services available to serve the communities; (iv) design and carrying out of all studies on economic, social, educational and cultural development; and (v) support to initiatives for decentralized cooperation. These missions are carried out free of charge for the local governments. However, the ARD may charge for project management services delegated to it by the local government.

The importance of regional and local development agencies in the decentralization implementation facility

Among the six countries synthesized here, only Senegal has local agencies established by law and the properties of the local authorities to operate in the area of project management support, ARDs. Under Article 37 of Act No. 96-06 establishing the ARD,[2] the regions jointly establish with the communes and rural communities an agency for supporting the development of member local governments. The local representatives of decentralized state services at the regional level are members of ARD's technical committee and participate in an advisory capacity in its board of directors.

The agencies depend on the obligatory contributions of member local governments for their operating funds, set each year by a joint decree of the Minister of Decentralization and the Minister of Finance, as well as subsidies, donations, bequests and resources generated by the services offered.

Compared to the Senegalese model, the Malian model is also focused on privatization of expert advisory services in the local authorities according to a project-type mechanism.

---

[2] At the moment of revising the summary, ARD received new missions to support the *Programme national de développement local* (PNDL)

Expert advisory services by the private sector in Mali

Technical support to local authorities in Mali is based on Community Advisory Centres (CAC) run by NGOs, development projects or research offices. Each CAC covers a cercle and its role is to support the communes in its local jurisdiction in project management of its local development. CAC's mission is to assist communes and provide them with technical assistance for project management in making investments, leading the activities of orientation committees and managing the database on local authorities.

The CACs are under a National Coordination Unit (NCU), which provides some degree of supervision in each region, known as regional monitoring. The entire facility comes under the authority of the National Office of Local Authorities through an agreement reached with the NCU.

The CAC facility is supported by an orientation facility ensuring coordination between the territorial approach and the sectoral approach in combating poverty:

- A National Orientation Committee (NOC), with an inter-ministerial profile, expanded into the National Local Authority Investment Agency (NLAIA), which is the financial component of the national facility to support local authorities, consular chambers, the *Association des maires du Mali* (MMA, Malian Mayors' Association) and NGO networks. The NOC aims to ensure the smooth operation of the CAC and create synergy among the projects of local authorities and sectoral programmes, and among the projects of different actors;

- A Regional Orientation Committee (ROC), comprises the governor, prefects, the Regional Assembly and the regional consular chambers. The ROC is a framework for monitoring and evaluation, and coordinating technical support related to the implementation of economic, social and cultural development plans in the region;

- A Local Orientation Committee (LOC) in each district comprises the prefect, communal councils, the district council, the local consular chambers and active NGOs. The LOC is an organization that approves CAC's work programme and monitors the implementation of their tasks.

1.4.5. Financial instruments and project management in local authorities

The civil service has a reputation of being not very *pre-active* (i.e. lacks planning capacity) and not very *pro-active* (has weak capacity to introduce desired changes). Decentralization also aims to undo this trend in routine management by promoting a dynamic of change based on predicting progress and investment programming in the medium and long terms—two essential preparatory conditions for success in delegating responsibility and directing local development.

a) Local planning for territorial governance of development

The planning of local development for a greater understanding of the populations' needs and the systemization of investment programming in the annual budgets of local authorities are considered an important emerging culture. More than just solving problems, all these development plans aim at making the most of local potential, an essential condition for generating wealth in order to combat poverty. Because of the significant contribution of local planning to the development process of local authorities, it has been expressly prescribed by the laws on decentralization of all the countries of the sub-region. Irrespective of the quality and feasibility of these plans, the planning exercise is of pedagogical, social and political interest because it is deemed by locally elected officials and their staff an important social mobilization event and an opportunity for debate on society projects, reflection and strategic choices on the future of the land and its people.

Planning is essential but its usefulness depends on mechanisms evaluating its role in the daily management of the local authorities and of initiatives of other categories of actors (public and private). In this start of the democratic and decentralization process, it is therefore essential that management of the local authority uses the opportunity of the increased user satisfaction to offer good quality and accessible services of general interest as per the millennium development goals (MDGs). To this end, performance assessment of locally elected officials in fulfilling their mandate is very important because it is part of local governance. Countries provide several mechanisms In this regard through collaboration frameworks, postings, and possibilities for citizens to attend regular communal council sessions as observers.

Planning to stimulate local initiatives

Planning is supported by performance indicators that should target the following levels or spheres of progress: the social dynamic linked to participation, economic stimulation by creating wealth; modernization by improving municipal administration to provide quality services within a reasonable time; self-motivated management by public services (education, health, water, telephone, electricity, sanitation); and environmental and natural resources protection.

Also, while financial criteria are essential, it is also essential to consider the quality of territorial governance as a whole, in particular: (i) *regular meetings* of the executive boards of technical commissions, *publication of the commune's accounts and posting of deliberations*; (ii) *the physical quality of products* and the maintenance *of infrastructure in operating order*; (iii) *restoration efforts* in degraded neighbourhoods and areas; (iv) the link between planning and annual *programme budgets*; (v) the functionality of spaces for *social dialogue* with local activists and neighbouring local authorities; (vi) the *level of revenue yields* against budget forecasts; the level of expertise in handling payroll and emoluments; and (vi) efforts *to invest own resources* and *to maintain facilities with own resources*.

b) Financial instruments to realise the investment programming

In exercising their authority, the local authorities must meet *operating expenses* (ordinary expenditures) and *investment expenses* (capital expenditures), the latter of which are far beyond local resource mobilization capacity. In fact, the locally elected officials are forced to turn to external resources such as public funding, grants, bequests, endowments set up by the State and loans. However, they can only rely for certain on two types of revenue to finance public expenditures even if they are far from consolidating financial independence: (i) *tax revenues*; and (ii) resources coming from *the price paid by clients (billing) in return for public goods and services* offered by the commune administration.

Most communes and rural communities have inherited an unbalanced and even catastrophic financial situation from the territorial administrative structures that preceded them. This situation affects the functionality, visibility and viability of local governments, in particular the most numerous ones in rural areas. With the exception of communes in large cities and to some extent in secondary towns with high demographic and economic potential, the financial situation of most communes is still precarious despite the various financial transfers from the State (support or incomes from rebates).

Support to decentralization and local authorities in each country is based on the creation of various financial instruments to strengthen institutional capacity and produce social, community and market infrastructure. These instruments are aided by various forms of bilateral and multilateral cooperation, including decentralized North-South cooperation. The partners with the highest profile in territorial policies are the European Union, the World Bank, the United Nations system (UNDP, UNCDF, UNICEF), the African Development Bank, the United States, Canada, Germany, France, Belgium, Denmark, Switzerland, and the Netherlands. The financial circuit adopted by programmes and projects in support of decentralization is almost identical, given that the same development partners are found in the six countries with the same cooperation policies. Their contributions can be grouped into three categories according to the circuits of financial flows:

- **Financial contributions through public accounting systems (budget support)**
  - Some projects have opened an dedicated account at the Public Treasury and the funding follows the classic circuit of public expenditure—i.e. *Projet d'Appui au Développement Communal et aux initiatives locales dans le Borgou* (ADECOI)/UNDP/UNCDF programme in Benin, *Programme d'Appui à la Décentralisation en Milieu Rural* (PADMIR) in Senegal, *Projets d'Appui aux Communes Rurales de Tombouctou et de Mopti* (PACR-T) in Mali through ANICT. This type of funding is the most in line with national decentralization procedures.
  - Specific funds are made available to communes to exercise their authority over project management. They are deposited in an account in the Treasury of the location concerned.
- **Financial contributions outside public accounting (parallel support)**
  - Other projects request the communes to systematically delegate their project management to an infra-communal level, particularly to a village development council or association. This is the case for some support programmes for decentralized rural development implemented under the poverty reduction strategy in Benin, Burkina Faso and Senegal, which are financed for infrastructure chosen by the communities.
- **Direct financial contributions to local authorities**
  - The local governments in Guinea can have their own bank account. Under the PDLG, the CRDs opened their own bank accounts, which has allowed them to manage directly the subsidies granted as UNCDF support.

Other contributions still require investments to be registered in local development plans to allow them to strengthen local project management (bidding process, project monitoring and control) by facilitating the double registration of the investment involved in the budget, and consequently, the necessary provision for their maintenance in the annual operating budgets. The financial circuit thus goes through the commune budget, bidding process and payments made by the public accountant. But generally, project management is delegated to executing agencies or project units.

On the impetus of some donors, such as the World Bank, project management delegated to a municipal agency tends to use a management approach, which is gaining strength in the institutional landscape of implementing decentralization in the sub-region. Some of the authorized agencies specialize in rural areas, others in urban areas, and still others, in both. Spatial specializations predominate in Senegal with, among others, the Commune Support Programme (CSP). All the programmes and agencies have allowed for experimentation with models of management and maintenance contracts for infrastructure in the health, education and water sectors, and for IGAs. Management of IGAs in certain countries was given back to local associations (school parents' associations, management committees, women's forums, societies for the protection of nature) by communal councils, under an agreement to delegate management for operation and maintenance.

Finally, government initiatives to aid decentralization and local development in local authorities may be summarized as two basic tools, *grant funds* and *agencies* funded by several financial backers (the State, local authorities, development partners), which are illustrated below by two examples from Senegal and Mali.

Since 1977 Senegal established the *Fonds d'équipement des collectivités locales* (FECL, Local Governments Capital Fund) for investment. The mission of this fund was to grant local authorities:

- no-interest loans to carry out their investments (not yet assigned to date);
- assistance funds.

In order to operate, FECL has resources (Articles 58 and 63 of Act No. 96-07 of 22 March 1996), which come from a levy on the VAT, whose rate is set each year by the Finance Act. The allocation committee meets periodically to revise requests submitted by local governments for assistance funds. The FECL allocates two types of funds: regular assistance funds and a special support fund. Regular assistance funds correspond to an endowment for facilities allocated to the local governments without designating a specific project. Their distribution among local governments is based on criteria of good management and aims at providing incentives for improving the return on their investment and streamlining their expenses. Once allocated, the regular assistance funds may be freely used by the local government on one condition — that they be used to finance investments. *Special public funding* is granted to local governments to allow them either to finance counterpart funds required by projects and programmes in support of decentralization, or to cover facilities expenses initiated by the State itself. *Special public funding* is also used to encourage rural communities to raise the level of rural tax collection. A rural community that collects 100 per cent of its rural tax benefits from special support funds of three million francs.

To supplement the FECL, Senegal has established a *Fonds de dotation de la décentralisation* (FDD, Decentralization Endowment Fund). The FDD, whose funding level is determined annually, is intended to compensate for operating expenses resulting from the transfer of powers to the local authorities. It is distributed on the basis of criteria for compensating local communities and for supporting decentralized administrations for the expert advisory services to those communities. At least 82 per cent of the total amount of the fund is distributed among the regions, the communes and rural communities; the regions receive an allocation not exceeding ten per cent of the overall endowment to cover operating expenses for their bodies. Finally, a fixed amount and a proportional amount according to the area and population of the regional administrative district are set aside for the state decentralized administrations to meet the requests of the local governments.

Mali has created the *Agence nationale d'investissement des collectivités territoriales* (ANICT, Local Authorities National Investment Agency), the financial component of the national facility to support local authorities. The Agency gives local authorities drawing rights aimed at supporting public investment, according to a selection and approval procedure for micro-projects that answers to the regional branch of ANICT in each region and its Regional Orientation Committee (ROC) headed by the governor. A similar fund is also planned for Benin (a Commune Development Support Fund), Burkina Faso (a Local Development Support Fund) and Niger (a Decentralization Support Fund).

Despite serious difficulties in transferring resources to local authorities, at times indicating an objective lack of state budget resources and often of political determination, state financial efforts are nevertheless growing steadily, but far from the minimum requirements of local communities to meet their potential. For the most part, resources are still retained and managed by the central level or entrusted to executing agencies. In sum, the transfer of competences and resources is still a major political challenge in poverty reduction strategies in all the countries of the sub-region where UNCDF is involved. According to one point of view, this situation is understandable considering the newness of the decentralization process, the fairly poor qualifications of most locally elected officials, and the lack of awareness among State agents regarding the issues involved in this state restructuring.

Other views are that the recentralization of resources through development agencies and projects is a logical result of the extreme political influence of local authorities and risks of misappropriation of objects of funding. Moreover, it is a pragmatic means to improving the absorption capacity of international assistance with the aim of raising the achievement level towards meeting the Millennium Development Goals.

1.5. Impact and main lessons learned

1.5.1. Main impact of decentralization on local and national dynamics

Towards diversification of social eligibility criteria

Decentralization is under way in the six countries, which convey a new awareness of the need to democratize the management of local affairs in order to improve the design and implementation of development programmes. Each local election is experienced as an evaluation exercise for locally elected officials to the point where they begin by integrating and referring their mandates to the necessary results underlying the communal competences. Although the first elections were essentially under the influence of the political parties, people are moving gradually towards diversifying the social criteria for eligibility based on moral values and the proven personal abilities of candidates running for local councillors.

Citizens' understanding of local taxation is growing. The elected officials know that there is a need to mobilize local resources and that it is essential for good governance and efficient performance. Even if the level of tax revenues is still low relative to its potential, the populations better integrate the role of taxes with decentralization than before.

Decentralization and development have become issues on which the development partners take action because they effectively contribute to achievement of MDGs and improving the level of consumption of international aid.

As a result of the culture of planning, today each commune knows its strengths, weaknesses and opportunities, and attempts to provide a chance for disadvantaged groups to access basic social services.

Even though participatory management and accountability are not yet automatic for all elected officials, some have truly made progress in communicating with civil society.

Consultative forum are formally prescribed by law. In all countries, therefore, the legislature is concerned with the need for territorial development (regional or local) to integrate other forms of legitimacy with which the people already identify in their areas. The various forum thus constitute a wise combination of *political legitimacy* (representativeness coming from the political class); *social legitimacy* (various associations coming from traditional chiefdom, cultural authorities, bodies of dominant professions such as rural agriculture, representatives of users of basic social services such as education, health and water supply); *technical legitimacy* (local representatives of decentralized state services, some networks of technical support NGOs); and *administrative and institutional legitimacy* (supervisory authority, executive offices of elected bodies).

All these experiences in community development through land use management programmes serve as a prerequisite for the entire decentralization process in the sub-region.

The current monopoly of expert advisory services exercised by local representatives of decentralized state services is in the process of disappearing to the benefit of liberalized support to local authorities with the emergence or consolidation of NGOs and local research offices that support them while learning on the field. The various capacity-building programmes in progress in each of the countries offer a real opportunity to a body of local expertise that will enable local elected officials to rely on the private sector to consolidate project management.

1.5.2. Main lessons learned on the institutional context and framework

Lesson 1: *Decentralization and local development should be encouraged as a means to achieve the Millennium Development Goals.*

- Local authorities raised many fears and questions among the local populations concerning the threat of tax pressure and the viability of communes. Today, decentralization is beginning to be adopted everywhere, both by locally elected officials and local populations as an opportunity to strengthen social and political dialogue, developing local dynamics and taking control over the development of each area. Decentralization, as a re-structuring process of the popular authority and promoting citizenry democracy, extends the area of local civil society around local community organizations (LCOs), which are already sowing the seeds of citizen control together with traditional control (administrative, political and legal).

- Administrative and financial autonomy, which constitutes the basic principle of decentralization, requires locally elected officials to communicate frequently with the population to gain their commitment for everyone's contribution to local development and maintaining the common good. Decentralization is an opportunity to raise local collective awareness of development problems and individual responsibility.

- Even though most communes depend on external aid, the fact that the local populations are beginning to understand the usefulness of decentralization is progress towards strengthening autonomy.

Lesson 2: *The transfer of competences to the local authorities is justified by the failure of State centralism and deepening poverty. However, these competences are too vast for current technical and financial capacities of locally elected officials and local governments.*

This situation has several causes:

- low managerial capacity among elected officials, many of whom are illiterate;
- poorly qualified, too scarce, insufficiently skilled and poorly motivated municipal staff (a high proportion are illiterate and unqualified) often maintaining authoritarian relationships with users;
- low local tax revenues and a low annual budget compared to missions of general interest;
- the lack of a local administration: it is confined to the community secretary (or general secretary of the mayor's office), a contracted agent or a state civil servant, generally a high school graduate, recruited and paid by the State;
- lack of political will to transfer power to the authority because of privileges and other advantages associated with management;
- lack of awareness of the opportunities offered by cooperation among communes. They are proud of their autonomy yet handicapped by political divergences or quarrels among the leadership, each local authority wanting all its own services to operate optimally, as provided by law. Although this desire seems legitimate, its feasibility is hampered by the lack of own resources and transfers. All the laws on decentralization allow cooperation among local authorities, but unfortunately, in reality, they are unaware of the opportunities offered by cooperation and the economies of scale that could result from sharing some services.

Lesson 3: *Insufficient consideration given to the concept of territory in the decentralization process and lack of political will to make decentralization a true opportunity to strengthen efficiency, effectiveness and impact of sectoral policies at the territorial level.*

This context is explained by the following facts and observations:

- **Lack of implementation texts for decentralization** laws to strengthen and expedite reform of territorial administration. Through ministerial departments, the fundamental structures continue to manage the implementation of, rather than define and monitor, national policies and other strategies. This institutional context can be explained by the glacial speed at which rules are made and laws implemented. Governors and prefects, who are supposed to be the agents of state authority at the regional and departmental level, only provide partial coordination of state actions. In effect, the state decentralized services define and implement their programme of activities more in relation to their sectoral hierarchies than the local authorities.

- **Lack Lack of linkages between the project portfolio identified, the local budget and the technical capacity of communes.** The implementation rates for these plans are very low due to being unrealistic, the lack of will by central governments and their low value in the national investment programming system. There are a variety of guidelines in each country and in the absence of a regulatory system providing a national framework harmonized with the national programming system, it becomes difficult to produce a regional and national synthesis of local development plans due to great variation in the basic structure.

- There are no **clear mechanisms** for switching from **state-imposed delegated project management** and certain development partners to **delegated project management chosen** to motivate elected local officials, especially to show them that they are stakeholders in an true process of transfer of competences and not in the re-centralization of a large part of their power for the benefit certain technical and financial support bodies.

- **Difficulty in coordinating and harmonizing regional development activities** among the region, the local authorities and the State.

- **Lack of a shared vision of local development** among the local authorities making up the same region, and almost no inter-communal cooperation initiatives among neighbouring communes.

- **The predominance of macroeconomic and sectoral policies over territorial policies.** States have difficulties in switching from a sectoral concept to a territorial concept where sectoral administrations would become the means for carrying out territorial development to serve local districts and local governments. Forecasting investment resources for the local authorities is managed by each ministry. The communes lack information on these State forecasts as they conduct local programming and planning exercises. Nevertheless, representatives of decentralized public services are present during the planning and programming process. Consequently, there are still major efforts needed to improve the flow of information in each sector in the local authority.

- **Possible improvements to frameworks and efforts for social dialogue on local and sectoral public policies.** In all laws on decentralization, coordination frameworks are expected to enable the participation of civil society organizations in defining and implementing development. It must be pointed out that the functioning of these cooperation and coordination frameworks is far from a priority in territorial budgets. Similarly, there is a lack of motivation and monitoring tools that would allow their value-added to be assessed. The civil society organizations also see themselves more as "police officers" and project operators than as a source of proposals, which hurts their credibility with locally elected officials who are already seeking the means to limit their influence.

- **Poor development of a culture of accountability.** This management approach is not yet routine; efforts should therefore be made to strengthen local governance.

- **Predominance of hierarchical relationships over supportive ones.** Many supervisory authorities have not yet understood the issues involved in decentralization and prefer to remain in control. This situation is aggravated even more in cases of co-territoriality than in institutional frameworks where the two types of powers are not superimposed over the same local area of authority. Unfortunately, capacity-building programmes are targeted more at locally elected officials than governors, prefects, sub-prefects and directors of local representatives of decentralized state services. This situation should be corrected.

- **Marginal integration of traditional chiefs in the institutional framework of decentralization.** Because of their historical legitimacy, the influence of traditional or religious chiefs is still significant in social control and popular expression, especially in rural areas. Although they cannot be ignored in any elections and are opinion-makers, in the name of democratic principles, the laws give them no place in the decision-making system. Nonetheless, it is in the interest of elected officials at the local level to have the traditional chiefs working with rather than against them.

- **Marginalization of civil society in the conquest of local power.** The extreme political aspect of local elections for community leadership is a discriminatory approach that does not recognize all those wishing to contribute their skills and make a personal commitment to managing their community. Control of local authorities by political parties represents key issues for national elections. But this politicization is often behind the instability and clashes within elected bodies, such as: the 2002 dissolution of the municipal and rural councils in favour of political change in Senegal; the series of discharges of mayors during the first two years of communization in Benin; and the dissolution of communal council to replace them with appointed mayors in Guinea. Further thinking on the issue of eligibility conditions for territorial advisors is needed in order to consolidate local participatory democracy and shelter it from political upheavals at the national level.

- **Lack of authority and capacity of the ministries responsible for local authorities.** While the governors or prefects should legally coordinate all sectoral interventions on the field on behalf of the State, project management for these programmes generally escapes the control of the ministries responsible for local governments. This situation is explainable by the fact that these ministries have traditionally been concerned more with security than with local and regional development. This lack of practice in directing development programmes and related procedures explains why many donors prefer to entrust supervision of their programmes to cross-cutting ministries such as finance and development. However, this mentality is changing and it was possible to place the ADECOI programme in Benin under the double administration of the ministries for decentralization and development.

- **The slow pace of land reform,** which fosters vagueness on the effective responsibilities of locally elected officials in land and natural resources management in general.

2] Projects in Support of Local Development Implemented by UNCDF and its Partners

2.1. History of the projects

The various programmes and projects implemented by UNCDF in partnership with UNDP and other donors are generally pilot projects supporting local development that prefigure decentralization, and more specifically communalization. Nine experiences are looked at in this study. The following programmes and projects are considered:

- **Benin:** ADECOI. Financing partners: UNDP, Belgian Survival Fund, Government of Benin and local governments.

- **Burkina Faso:** *Projet de développement des Ressources Agropastorales de la Province du Namentenga* (PAPNA, Namentenga Province Agro-pastoral Resources Development Project) and *Projet d'Appui au Programme Sahel Burkinabé* (PSB, Sahel Burkinabe Programme Support Project) in Soum Province. Financing partners: UNDP, Belgian Survival Fund, Government of Burkina Faso and the populations of the target areas.

- **Guinea:** *Programme de Développement Local en Guinée* (PLDG, Local Development Programme in Guinea). Financing partners: UNDP, Government of Guinea and local governments.

- **Mali:** PACR/TM. Financing partners: UNDP, Belgian Survival Fund, Luxembourg, Government of Mali and local governments.

- **Niger:** Local Development Support Projects (PADLs) at N'Guigmi and Mayahi. Financing partners: UNDP, Belgian Survival Fund, Government of Niger and the population of the target areas.

- **Senegal:** Rural Support Programme (PADMIR). Financing partners: UNDP, European Union, Luxembourg, Government of Senegal and local governments.

Most of these projects either follow previous interventions focused on an eco-development approach dating back to the 1990s, or interventions of the last generation, directed more towards supporting decentralization and local development. Previous projects included: (i) *Projet d'Appui au Développement Local dans le Borgou-Est et l'Atacora-Ouest* (PADEL, Support to Local Development in East Bourgou and West Atacora Project) in Benin; (ii) *Projet d'Actions de Production et d'Accompagnement dans le Namentenga* (PAPANAM, the Production and Assistance Project in Namentenga), *Projet de Construction de la Route Boulsa-Tougouri* (the Boulsa-Tougouri Road Construction Project), *Projet d'Appui au Programme Sahel Burkinabé* (PA-PSB phase 1, the Sahel Burkinabe Support Project) in Burkina Faso; (iii) *Programme d'Appui au Programme de Développement Rural de la Moyenne Guinée* (PPDR/MG, the Support Programme for the Middle Guinea Rural Development Programme), *Programme d'Appui à la Gestion des Terroirs Villageois du Séno-Gondo* (the Support Programme for the Seno-Gondo Village Land Use Programme) and *Programme de Pérennisation des Systèmes Rizicoles dans les régions de Gao et de Tombouctou au Mali* (the Rice Cultivation Programme in the Gao and Timbuctu regions of Mali).

There are three categories of projects making up the UNCDF interventions in West Africa at the time, resulting from an analysis of their location and their objectives:

- **Eco-development projects**, which placed great importance on natural resources management and environmental protection through most of the operational components of interventions, while also addressing poverty eradication.

- **Rural development projects,** which gave priority to food security as a sector where the promoted actions were concentrated.

- **Local development projects,** which are based on a more comprehensive approach, putting the commune structure at the centre of the intervention. They were inherently both: (i) institutional, by strengthening the role and capacities of the various local actors and promoting participatory democracy; (ii) planning-related, by establishing socio-collective infrastructure and equipments; and (iii) economic, by diversifying IGAs for the population and for the local territorial administration through the mobilization of tax resources.

Village micro-projects were the core of the local rural development strategy in all of these different interventions that are part of the recent history of UNCDF-led projects carried out in West Africa. They should not be perceived as a simple exercise in building infrastructure; the focus should be on the concept of local public services that this infrastructure offers to the citizens of these areas.

Objectives of previous generations of UNCDF projects

Projet d'Appui au Développement Local dans le Borgou-Est et l'Atacora-Ouest (PADEL, Support to Local Development in East Bourgou and West Atacora Project) in Benin

(i) to improve the living conditions of the population and revitalize economic growth at the grassroots level by setting up an appropriate financing tool; (ii) increase the capacities for initiatives and management In local authorities in local economic and social life; (ii) promote micro-business by providing access to appropriate financial services

Projet d'Actions de Production et d'Accompagnement dans le Namentenga (PAPANAM, the Production and Assistance Project in Namentenga) in Burkina Faso

(i) make agriculture more secure by controlling water and increase agricultural production; (ii) improve the populations' supply and nutrition of basic cereals; and (iii) promote self-development through the land use management approach.

Projet d'Appui au Programme Sahel Burkinabé (PA-PSB, the Sahel Burkinabe Support Project) in Burkina Faso

(i) help to combat against desertification and implement agricultural and land reorganization; (ii) support the institutional strengthening of *Commissions Inter-Villageoises de Gestion de Terroir* (CIVGT, inter-village land management committees) in order to transform them into structures for stimulation and management of local development.

PDRMG in Guinea

Programme d'Appui au Programme de Développement Rural de la Moyenne Guinée (PPDR/MG, the Support Programme for the Middle Guinea Rural Development Programme)

Improve the living conditions of farmers in a sustainable manner by increasing their income through the integration of the agricultural sector into the national economic policy.

Poverty Reduction Strategy Paper (PRSP) in Mali

(i) perpetuate production systems; (ii) give autonomy to representation structures and development operators; (iii) promote banking and credit in rural areas; (iv) promote diversification of production activities, especially for women.

Kédougou LDF in Senegal

Improve living conditions for the poorest groups through eco-development and the local development fund and income-generating activities, especially to benefit women's groups.

Overall, these micro-projects are an important source for improving living conditions and production systems. They have enabled experimentation and promotion of technical progress in agriculture, forestry and livestock farming, as well as stimulated local economies by supporting microfinance and IGSs, especially for women's groups.

One constant in all these micro-projects is the aid provided to rural communities for adopting democratic and participatory decision-making processes, preparing them to better protect their interests within the administrations in charge of development issues, while working in harmony for the higher interests of their community.

It should be noted that apart from Senegal where PADMIR was already linked with rural councils, decentralization has not been effective in the other countries. The implementation of these projects resulted in the establishment of village and inter-village land use committees serving as frameworks for local populations to take responsibility for local planning, resources mobilization, contracting, monitoring of projects and allocating work. The three types of projects show some essential and common characteristics that should be highlighted:

a) **Local project management** of project activities at each community according to the concept of making the entire community responsible, leading and making all the decisions within the community on access to social and community services in the education, health, and water sectors, as needed. The key issue here is allowing the institutions and organizations responsible for decision-making to be as close as possible to the populations concerned. This institutional characteristic of support projects resulted in support to capacity building through training in group dynamics, planning-programming and contracting management, together with community monitoring and evaluation and accounting—everything related to the learning of the roles and responsibilities of a deliberating body of a local government. For certain projects, this dynamic was part of a strategy to prepare for decentralization.

b) **Natural resource management and environmental protection:** Almost all the areas of UNCDF intervention are undergoing difficult environmental conditions marked by problems of rainfall, degradation of land and forest resources, and lack of pasture for cattle. These areas are often faced with frequent conflicts between farmers and livestock breeders. Food deficit and malnutrition are recurrent situations affecting the development of these areas. Stabilization of family farms and food security requires actions in soil protection and restoration, rural water supply, promotion of village forestry, and integration of agriculture, livestock farming and reforestation into production systems.

c) **Development of IGAs:** Monetary poverty is a dominant characteristic of all the intervention areas. Its excessive influence over food security, children's schooling, access to health care and mobilization of local tax resources for community investment no longer need to be demonstrated. The response seems to require the establishment of credit lines and loan security funds from the banking and microfinance structures to support small promoters. However, these practices have been modified to take into account the lessons learned and best practices in microfinance.

d) **Improved social-community services offered through co-financing:** This is particularly relative to infrastructure and facilities for primary education, adult education, community health, village water supply, sanitation and opening to the outside world. A financial mechanism (the Local Development Fund) supports these services, which also permits financing of commercial facilities and infrastructure, in particular, warehouses and market stalls, stores, slaughterhouses and butcheries, *inter alia*, from which taxes were collected by local administrations. Support was also provided in some cases to bring some villages with production potential out of isolation.

e) **The gender approach** (advancing the status of women), **the participatory approach** (contracting and accountability), integration of marginalized groups (lower castes) and land use management for the **fair share of investments** among the communities on the basis of social dialogue and consensus in the framework of a planning process.

2.2. Characteristics of projects capitalized

2.2.1. Characteristics of intervention areas

General characteristics

UNCDF prefers to intervene in the most vulnerable and poorest areas. This choice is in perfect harmony with its mandate, which aims to reduce poverty by implementing local development programmes.

The project intervention areas have the following geographical characteristics: (i) they are very far removed from the capitals of the countries of intervention (up to 1,500 km in N'Guigmi, Niger); (ii) they are located in areas with low rainfall or right at the gateway of the Sahel and subject to recurring ecological and food crises; and (iii) they have very high agricultural potential but are isolated and poorly developed as in the intervention areas of Benin and Guinea.

All the projects are linked with decentralization and support local governments and local organizations. They cover a significant number of rural development communes, from seven in Benin to 23 in Guinea and 134 in Mali.

Major problems leading to the selection of each area

The consolidation of prior UNCDF interventions in each of these countries and the need to assist the decentralization process in its strategies to combat poverty justify the choice of the areas as a whole. However, each intervention area is part of the poorest areas in its country, whose vulnerability can be explained by some of the following structural features.

Benin

- 50 per cent of the population in the intervention zone lives below the poverty threshold;
- Poverty has many forms: (i) households face difficulty in meeting their food costs during the dry season, lasting four to six months, aggravating the problems of child malnutrition; (ii) school enrolment rates are very low; (iii) women have a heavy work burden; (iv) farmers sell cropland to compensate for the drop in income.

Burkina Faso

- The weakness of development interventions in the area and their low level of development compared to other provinces in the country

Guinea

- A worrisome social situation: (i) very limited access to basic services; (ii) a very low school enrolment rate, especially among girls; (iii) around 70 per cent illiteracy rate among the population; and (iv) isolation of production areas.

Mali

- Around 76 per cent of the population of Mopti and Timbuctu live below the poverty threshold.

Niger

- The departments of N'Guigmi and Mayahi are extremely vulnerable with regard to their geographical location, which exposes them to recurring ecological and economic crises.

- Factors of vulnerability: (i) the illiteracy rate has reached 80 per cent; (ii) poor performance of agricultural tools and equipment, (iii) decline in soil fertility and chronic food crises; and (iv) lack of and mediocre socio-economic infrastructure (schools, healthcare centres, water systems and roads).

Senegal

- A dire lack of infrastructure and facilities for health, education and water supply: (i) the deficit in quantity and quality of health centres and 44 per cent of the population without access to health infrastructure within five km; (ii) a high proportion of schools in temporary shelters (flimsy materials), without sanitation facilities, enclosing walls and water points; the schools do not meet the required quality standard; and (iii) difficult access to water, usually provided by wells in rural areas.

From all these characteristics and problems described above, the choice of intervention areas was determined by their very low level of development: (i) hunger and malnutrition; (ii) monetary poverty; (iii) the production base in rural areas relying on depleted natural resources; (iv) adult illiteracy and a low rate of school enrolment for children; (v) difficulty in access to safe drinking water and healthcare; (vi) low level of social and community investments and deplorable conditions of hygiene and sanitation; and (vii) lack of institutional and organizational capacity to promote local development.

2.2.2. Project objectives

The development objectives of the UNDP/UNCDF projects are generally almost identical and based on the characteristics and problems discussed above. They deal with the sustainable improvement of livelihoods of rural populations through a system of local programming and multi-sectoral investments.

The immediate objectives relate to: (i) improving food security; (ii) building capacities of society organizations, local governments and local representatives of decentralized state services; (iii) assisting decentralization and improving local governance for sustainable human development in rural communities; (iv) improving the well-being of the populations through IGAs and promoting local economic development; and (v) improving the facilities, infrastructure and delivery of basic social services and the decentralized management of natural resources.

2.2.3. Approaches and methods of intervention

The objectives of projects founded on combating poverty and promoting sustainable human development are put into operation through procedures that can be summarized through several elements of the profile found in every project.

Principles of intervention

Assistance to the decentralization process and support to local development by experimental programmes and projects—carried out by UNCDF in partnership with the UNDP and its other financial partners—follow a set of fundamental principles.

- **Decentralization and project management of local development**: Projects help combat poverty by homogenous support (methodological, technical, financial, delegation of decision-making power, etc.) to local actors, in particular to transitional local institutions (IVLUC and CMC), and specifically, to local governments if set up. The projects aim to make a concrete contribution to discussions on the implementation of decentralization.

- **Subsidiarity and learning by doing approach**: Subsidiarity affirms that all operations should be entrusted as close as possible to the grassroots level due to comparative advantage. Subsidiarity is a main strategic focus to the extent that it allows a partnership with all local actors — civil society organizations, rural organizations, NGOs and producers' groups — to learn how to decide on and implement their current development activities in an efficient manner.

- **Strategic partnership**: As part of a sustainable strategy for financing and implementing local development, all projects prefer taking initiatives to establish collaborative relationships with institutional partners (projects, government institutions, national and international NGOs, local associations) that are already active or plan to get started in the intervention area.

- **Cofinancing of micro-projects** with local contributions in various forms as a way to demonstrate appropriation, the will, commitment and sustainability of the supply of services produced. It places special focus on the financial contribution of the communal institution.

- **Transparency:** Sharing Information sharing on the management of development activities and as a means of strengthening both social dialogue on local policies and citizen participation in the management of local affairs and social control.

- **Requirements of accountability:** The duty of each institutional actor to account for his or her actions to the other stakeholders as a method of results-based management, verifying user satisfaction and taking into account the interests of poor and marginalized groups and minorities.

- **Capitalization:** Projects capitalize on lessons learned, particularly in the participation of all actors in decision-making processes, transparency in management of development activities, and the accountability requirement.

Intervention strategies incorporating these principles

- **A local planning system** as an iterative participation process and a programming mechanism for priority actions affecting several villages and allocating responsibility to different actors for the project management of development activities;

- **A Local Development Fund** adapted to the realities of the regions, making managed financing accessible with the help of decentralized mechanisms;

- **Project financing** in line with national procedures for decentralization;

- **Experimenting with organizing stakeholders** to strengthen dialogue and collective actions (communal development committees, communal contracting commissions, inter-village land use committees);

- **A withdrawal strategy** through inter-village committees and the communal institutions that will take over the project to consolidate achievements in each field of investment.

- **A review of lessons learned** in order to inform and influence national policies at both the legislative and instrumental levels.

Supports to formalization of the strategy

The intervention strategy is formalized through essential documents that are common to all intervention projects. These documents are set up by the communities and local governments together with the projects' support In order to promote of local development:

- **A partnership agreement** between each local government and the project defining the financial commitments of the parties, roles and responsibilities and performance criteria;

- A five-year general **local development plan**;

- A multi-year investment programme (MIP) over three years;

- An annual investment programme (AIP);

- **Contracts for activities** to assign responsibilities and accountability requirements;
- **Technical execution and financial reports** at varying intervals; in all cases, an annual report is obligatory and must specify activities carried out.

Typology of activities financed

There are two groups of micro-projects financed by projects:

- **Micro-projects under communal project management:** social-community infrastructure under the supervision of the commune;
- **Micro-projects managed by grassroots groups:** Projects carried out by groups of women's organizations, generally concerned with reducing women's burdens or IGAs, such as mills, village grain banks, or supply stores for village associations.

Several dimensions are revealed by the intervention approach to UNCDF/UNDP projects:

- **Political dimension:** linked to better governance at the State and local governments level;
- **Social and cultural dimension:** based on raising the basic level of infrastructure and the quality of services delivery essential to the well-being of the population;
- **Economic dimension:** relating to the promotion of local economic development through IGAs and strengthening of market infrastructure;
- **Environmental dimension:** relating to sustainable management of natural resources, land use planning and environmental protection.

Financial contributions

Financing is based on co-financing (see 3.4). Most of the interventions carried out by UNCDF in Africa are financed by UNDP/UNCDF, Luxembourg Cooperation, and the European Union, on the one hand, and African Governments, local governments, microfinance institutions and direct beneficiaries, on the other. The budget mobilized per project is in the range of 4 to 12.6 million USD.

2.3. Frameworks for coordination and partnership

Institutional partnerships consist of: (i) governmental structures: central ministries and decentralized administrations; (ii) local governments; (iii) private bodies: NGOs and research institutes that operate activities in partnership with project management teams in the communes; (iv) village associations and groups; and (v) some development projects interested in collaboration. The UNCDF/UNDP intervention areas have increasingly become a focus of the United Nations system agencies in each country.

In general, the project coordination framework involves the following institutional arrangements:

An anchor ministry with an incorporated focal point, usually the central office in charge of research, forecasting and planning. Technical and administrative supervision of each project is provided according to the project by the Ministry of Agriculture, Water and Fish Resources (in the case of PAPNA in Burkina Faso), the Ministry of Decentralization and Territorial Administration (ADECOI in Benin, PDLG in Guinea, PACR in Mali and PADMIR in Senegal), the Ministry of Finance, the Economy and Development (in the case of PADL in Niger) and the Ministry of the Environment (the case of PA/PSB in Burkina Faso).

The tripartite review, which is the decision-making body and serves as a steering committee for the project, is responsible for approving annual investment plans and annual implementation reports. It is responsible for deciding on the direction for the project, along with its revisions, continuation and termination. It includes government representatives (all the technical ministries involved, including finance and development), donor representatives (UNDP/UNCDF), representatives of local populations, and the project management unit.

The projects' technical cooperation framework regional cooperation and coordination framework for development activities. This framework can be specific to one project or be a permanent local framework for cooperation and coordination used by all the projects of the region concerned. It is presided over by the supervisory authority of the project intervention area. According to the administrative organization of the country, the authority may be the regional governor, high commissioner or prefect of the department. All the decentralized state services concerned and the project management unit are part of the framework, which aims to promote the circulation of information among all actors in the region. In so doing, field activities would be harmonized, taking into consideration the national and regional outlines for land use management.

The operational partnership includes all the development projects, NGOs and local associations operating in similar or complementary fields in the same intervention area. Generally, the partnership concerns actors working on land use planning programmes, food security, basic infrastructure development, rural extension and adult training, IGAs and microfinance. Thus, at the local level, the primary partners of projects are communal councils and mayors, village land use committees, and inter-village or communal commissions/committees on land management.

2.4. Innovations promoted
Organizational dynamic and structuring of the environment

The situation has gone from one where only traditional chiefs, local administrations and local representatives of decentralized state technical services reflected on, decided and carried out activities on behalf of the rural communities, to one characterized by the emergence of new actors creating new decision-making processes by means of the village and inter-village councils, and communal councils. These councils now act in the name of and on behalf of the general interest of the local populations, to whom they are accountable.

The local planning process and its implementation costs

The local planning process and its implementation costs depend on major involvement by the population through cooperation mechanisms, surveys, decision-making and implementation of programmed actions.

The communes, village and inter-village committees, and the social and professional organizations (women's groups, and livestock farmers' and farmers' associations) provide frameworks for participation in planning, while at the same time, serve as channels of communication and mobilization.

Principal difficulties related to planning

The planning process, while certainly participatory, is very lengthy and not easily replicated by local bodies, particularly due to the expanse of some communes and their lack of own transportation, the complexity of diagnostic and planning tools (numerous questionnaires, voluminous documents published in French), and the low educational level of stakeholders and the general population. Planning also creates very high expectations that financing mechanisms are incapable of fully meeting. There is a major gap, therefore, between expectations and the capacity to implement the identified priority actions. This creates a danger that the populations may become disillusioned with the participatory planning process.

The most important contributions come from village committees, groups and social and professional organizations, thus turning the preparation process of the communal development plan into a participatory exercise carried out by the communities themselves with the support of the assisting technical services and NGOs.

The highly participatory planning/programming system allows for a gradual and endogenous emergence of a spirit of openness, tolerance and solidarity of VLUCs and IVLUCs. This change in behaviour prepares communities for an inter-community dynamic and a culture of peace that will open up opportunities for implementing large-scale projects of common interest with economies of scale in several fields. The experience of the local planning process in the UNCDF projects (see table 2) shows an average production cost of the Plan de développement communal (CDP, Communal Development Plan) between 131 FCFA and 190 FCFA per capita on the basis of the data from three countries—Benin, Guinea and Senegal. This cost includes all the instruments implemented in the first year of the project, the Local Development Plan (a five-year duration), the Multi-Year Investment Plan (three years) and the Annual Investment Plan (over one year).

Table 2: Average production costs of community development plans

Country	Number of communes	Population	Total cost	Average cost per commune	Cost per capita
Benin	7	500,000	65,760,908 CFAF	9 million CFAF	131 CFAF/person
Guinea	23	375,000	71,300,000 CFAF	3.1 million CFAF	190 CFAF/person
Senegal	26	455,000	78,000,000 Fcfa	3,0 million CFAF	171 CFAF/person

A cost over 200 CFAF per person would be difficult for the community to absorb. It is important, therefore, to determine the cost of planning per person because it would allow to make these costs relative for the budget periods.

Preventive management of rural conflicts through communal land commissions: defining the boundaries of spaces for public use (grazing areas) by these structures that represent the appropriate forum for preventive management of rural conflicts, in particular, those related to natural resources utilization.

Protection of the environment and natural resources management: making cooperation frameworks responsible for essential functions such as the regeneration, protection and conservation of natural resources has helped to compensate for gaps in the official state system in this area.

Contracting: Competition and contractualization

The creation of communal contracting commissions is aimed at devolving the procedures for awarding public contracts, which up to now has been perceived as a duty of central power and territorial representatives of the State (governors, high commissioners, prefects, sub-prefects). Moreover, contracting through a bidding process, and when necessary, through consultation that is restricted but still open to multiple candidates, has introduced new reactions, methods and perceptions towards public management at the community level. This places transparency at the centre of management of local general interests.

Furthermore, in their management practices, locally elected officials call for open competition or competition restricted to local or even national operators through tenders that they open publicly according to the rules. They decide on how to award the contracts for the projects whose implementation they monitor.

The contracting committees at the IVLUC have developed many innovative bid request procedures and restricted consultation by separating bids for supplies from those for services in regard to infrastructure contracts. This initiative has led to significant progress in controlling supplies and managing stocks, including monitoring materials at the worksite. This is an important step forward for communities with low literacy.

The local development financing system based on the commune budget: Important innovations leading to progress in local governance and poverty reduction are: the mobilization of the total amount of state counterpart funds and communes through a levy at the source by the Public Treasury; management of counterpart funds (State and commune) by the commune; and the lack of in-kind counterpart funds demanded from the populations in order to gradually establish a local taxation culture.

Expenditure circuit through national public finance: This is the circuit of transfer of funds from the Public Treasury which is used for the financial execution of LDF. UNCDF has made available the necessary funds on the basis of the decision of the steering and financing allocation committee. The funds were then transferred into a special account in the Public Treasury. This experiment is in the process of building the credibility of the State, by showing that certain public financial administrations are capable of managing project funds efficiently and transparently, which are resources whose use follows a strict programming for consumption and according to precise objectives. Today, this experiment is attracting many development partners.

Disbursement circuit through national public finance: This is the funds transfer circuit from the Public Treasury, which is used for the financial implementation of LDF. UNCDF made the necessary funds available on the basis of decisions by the steering and financing allocation committee. The funds were then transferred into a special account in the Public Treasury. This experimentation is in the process of building the State's credibility by showing that certain public financial administrations are capable of managing project funds efficiently and transparently, which are resources used according to strict consumption programming and precise objectives. Today, this experiment is attracting many development partners.

Community management of collective infrastructure through a participatory technical control system: The creation of specific committees responsible for managing collective infrastructure and facilities represents a new approach aimed at allocating greater responsibility to rural communities and guaranteeing ownership and sustainability of investments, whose renewal is still well beyond current local abilities.

Confidence in decentralization: Within the framework of UNCDF projects, there is a real desire to trust the institutions set up through decentralization policies, since it is through the consolidation of the communes that decentralization will survive and succeed. It is a matter of shifting from a project logic to a concept of institutional sustainability and therefore to prove that decentralization operates through a learning by doing approach (for example, the Treasury circuit, project management by the local governments and the management committees).

Some constraints to be highlighted are:

- **In-kind counterparts are difficult to manage for local authorities.** Operators or entrepreneurs can use problems with quantity or quality as an excuse not to take responsibility for project manager. Furthermore, when manpower is provided by the community, it is not always available when desired, which causes major delays in building infrastructure, once again taking responsibility away from the entrepreneur.

- **The functioning of infrastructure is not always guaranteed.** Despite prior commitments by both sides, additional investments promised by others are not always delivered and the staff promised by the State are not made available to the communities.

- **Management practices are poor in some communes,** such as holding back payments to enterprises either by mayors or state agents. These practices cause major short-changes as well as delays in building infrastructure.

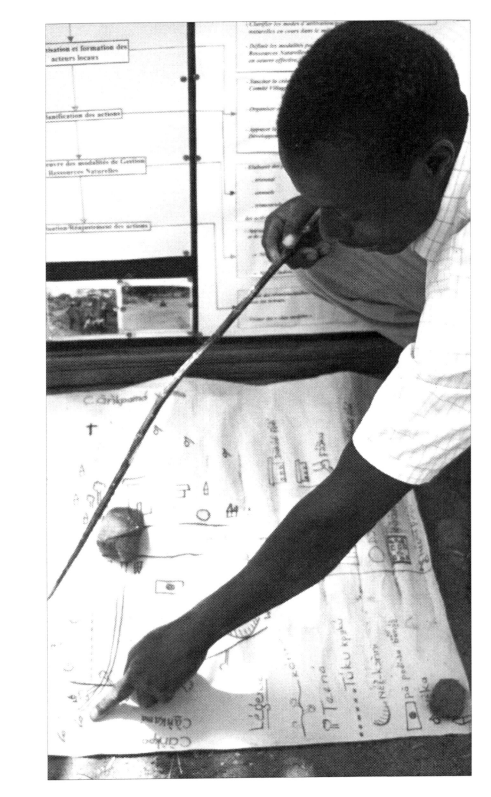

3] METHODOLOGICAL APPROACHES

3.1. Instruments and the local planning cycle

UNCDF support to decentralization and local development includes systematic support to establishing local planning instruments. UNCDF agreements to support a local government or commune thus include local planning and related assistance efforts, in particular, the strengthening of the technical and institutional capacity of local actors to lead the planning—budgeting process and co-financing implementation of part of the instalments of the annual local development plans. To this end, and in accordance with the legal framework of decentralization in each country, a communal facility is set up, either a communal development commission or an inter-village land use committee.

3.1.1. Instruments and principles of communal and local development planning

Communal or local planning is a territorial management approach, requiring results-based management to channel investments and streamline the use of resources mobilized for the benefit of the local populations and future generations. Its objective is to raise awareness among locally elected officials and local populations on the future of their territory in terms of local development, poverty reduction and reducing inequality. Such a direction counters the lack of efforts in programming and mobilizing local investment resources for annual budgets. The commune's budget should therefore be an annual instrument for implementing the commune's development plan.

Main planning instruments

As mentioned in the section on supports to formalizing the strategy, the planning exercise produces three documents in UNCDF partner communes:

- *The communal development plan (CDP)* or *local development plan (LDP),* which is a guidance tool and a long-term framework generally covering a five-year period;
- *The multi-year investment programme (MIP),* which makes CDP operational through a sliding programming of investment needs and resources to be mobilized over the next three years;

- *The annual investment programme (AIP),* which serves as a programme budget for the year and allows implementation of the CDP according to a results-based approach. This approach results in an annual performance evaluation in the commune to evaluate the achievement of local development objectives.

Through these different support tools and local development management, new orientations and impetus can be given to local authorities, particularly local governments (communes), which from now on has to be very close to their citizens and offer services to meet their expectations. To accomplish this, the commune cannot be concerned with its own operations alone nor, as in the past, fail to involve themselves in resolving local development problems of each community. The commune thus needs to manage the local population's demands for public services, local economic potential, their capacity to contribute, and ways and means to increase the commune's investment capacity to meet investment expenditure. In sum, the mobilization of local resources is essential to lay the foundations for sustainable local development. For this reason, UNCDF projects stress the need to take into consideration local resource mobilization efforts in the communes' annual performance evaluation.

Local development plans or communal development plans can be understood, therefore, as economic, social and cultural development plans incorporating environmental concerns and a gender dimension.

Some main principles of local planning

The principles of communal project management are observed by UNCDF projects once the communes are established.

Prior to decentralization and on an experimental basis, these principles were used by inter-village land use commissions or committees. Other principles, which are based on decentralization laws, can be identified on local planning:

1. The commune provides project management of the planning process management.

2. Planning process should be prepared by informing the populations extensively on major issues and by training the actors who will provide leadership at various levels: communal councillors and agents, technical services of decentralized state services in the region, community leaders and contractors/service providers of the services involved.

3. The planning process is participatory, i.e. all the components of the commune (villages, sections, subdivisions and various organizations) are consulted by the communal authorities.

4. Development actors working in the commune should take part in the planning process.

5. The drafting of the communal development plan takes into account both the needs of the people and state sectoral policies.

6. Development plans should express a long-term vision for local development that is not conditional on the term of office of its elected officials. The development objectives, projects and activities arising from this vision should convey a will to integrate all the local communities and social groups into the local development process.

7. The annual programmed budget is derived from the multi-year investment programme.

8. The local development plan is the tool for coordination and coherence for all public and private interventions that must operate within the territory of the local government.

9. In addition to its own interests, the local development plan takes into account shared interests with neighbouring communities in order to promote cooperation among communities and good neighbourly relationships.

3.1.2. Communal development planning cycle

The planning cycle includes three main phases: (i) preparation, (ii) planning; and (iii) programming and implementation. These phases are divided into nine stages, which are not compartmentalized, but interconnected at the operational level.

Preparation Phase

1. Establishment of a steering committee and a wide public information campaign on the mayor's initiative.

   - This stage allows to set up all the organizational structures necessary for the preparation of the development plan. It defines the terms of reference and work progress schedule. Mainly, it provides explanation of major issues in the communal development plan and the importance of wide mobilization among the local populations in its design.

   - The planning process entails the establishment of a steering committee, if not in place already, generally headed by the mayor or one of his deputies. The committee draws up the communal development plan. Its representation within the commune helps to organize and mobilize the populations and lead village assemblies and panels within the communities in order to diagnose problems and seek solutions.

- The communal planning commission is made up of locally elected officials and resources persons assigned to the development projects, the decentralized state services and NGOs working within the community. Leaders are trained within the community and available to village development committees and inter-village committees to help them organize village assemblies to conduct diagnoses, make proposals and define their priority needs.

- A planning guide serves as a support to guide the process and train members of various committees on what is needed to assist the planning process.

- The definition and mobilisation of the budget to implement the planning process.

- This stage relies on a variety of channels for communication: local radio, traditional communicators (*griots*), leaders of public opinion, heads of civil society organizations, administrative bulletins and supervision tours made by locally elected officials.

2. Inventory of available documentation and agents in the commune.

- Primary data collection among commune officials, technical services, administrative authorities, development projects, eminent persons and other local resources persons on: (i) the prevailing situation in various sectors of economic, social and environmental concern; (ii) investments planned by the public administration and development projects for the commune; (iii) the list of the various stakeholders involved in the commune and their field of activity.

- Processing and analysis of the above data for a better understanding of the information, which must be collected in the subsequent stages (diagnostic/proposals by local communities).

- **Outcome of the stage:** relevant documentation gathered and analysed by sector and location (intermediate level between the commune and the village) according to the availability of information.

Planning Phase

3. Diagnosis/ participatory proposals at the community level.

- Participatory diagnosis (PD) sessions at the village, inter-village and commune levels are held. PDs aim to identify potential and assets, problems, needs and aspirations of each village and commune. At each level, the priorities are determined on the basis of three questions: (i) What problems are obstacles to development? (ii) What problems seriously affect the villages as a whole?

(iii) What problems can the people solve themselves? This questioning guides the community management system and the means to reach those goals. Data is collected in assemblies by panels composed according to type and/or local development topic within the communities, and in workshops with technical working groups at the commune level. The same organization is used during the other phases as needed.

- In order to refine the diagnosis, some UNCDF support projects, particularly in Mali and Benin, have used a system of financial and institutional analysis in the communes based on three types of audits: (i) *institutional and organizational audit*, which drafts a status report on the functioning of communal services, evaluates the technical abilities of their human resources and the quality of services provided to the populations, and analyses citizen participation and their level of knowledge and awareness on the public affairs of the commune. The institutional and organizational audit results in the drafting of an institutional and organizational capacity-building programme for the commune; (ii) *financial audit*, which focuses on tax assessment, inventories, roles, issuances collections, the budget and fixed expenditures of the community. The financial audit results in a plan of action for the economic recovery of the local authority; and (iii) *audit of the local economy*, which is an analysis of promising economic prospects. It identifies potential, opportunities and constraints on economic activity. The audit aims to build community capacities for their financial contribution to local development. The audit of the local economy concludes with a draft plan of action on local economy development.

- **Outcome of the stage:** (i) the main resources and potential are identified; (ii) major problems are identified; and (iii) a census and analysis of local communities' needs and aspirations, inter-village needs, and needs on a communal scale, particularly of the communal administration, are determined.

4. Definition of orientations, objectives and strategic focal points for development.

   - Participatory planning begins with a meeting to report on the results of participatory diagnosis (PD). Solutions identified during the PDs are turned into concrete orientations and projects in the short, medium and long term, covering the territory concerned. The results of this process give structure to the local development plan (LDP).

- **Outcome of the stage:** This stage generates the local or communal development plan. It encompasses the vision, global and specific development objectives, the strategic areas of concentration, and the priority types of projects and development activities decided by the communal council. The results of all the stages in this phase are reported to the population through village assemblies.

Programming and Implementation Phase

5. Triennial programming.
   - The main projects and activities that must structure each strategic area are identified and are subject to a feasibility review through cost estimates and analysis of the commune's ability to mobilize resources. The scheduling and spatial planning of the activities over the next three years follows.
   - **Outcome of the stage:** Spatial planning and scheduling of the projects and activities is carried out and the financing plan is designed. The implications of the multi-year programme for the communal institution and local communities in terms of organization and means to mobilize are examined so that each component of local society would already know what efforts they have to make towards achieving the development plan objectives. An update is provided on the lack of resources that should be sought by the government and development partners, which represent the most important aspect. The results of this phase are reported to the community.
   - **Outcome of the stage:** The draft development plan and the multi-year investment programme are endorsed by the communal commission, guiding the process leading to the development plan.

6. Adoption and approval of the development plan and the multi-year investment programme.
   - The communal council adopts the two planning documents and then submits them to the supervisory authority for approval. Both tools can be submitted in a single document or separately. Approval is generally the responsibility of a cooperation and coordination framework for development activities above the commune level (cercle, province, department, region, etc.), which, according to the country, is headed either by the prefect, the governor or the high commissioner. This commission, which includes the supervisory authority, locally elected officials, and occasionally, representatives

of civil society, is responsible for ensuring that plans cohere with national policy and conform with regional land use development plans.

- **Outcome of the stage:** The communal council deliberates on the development plan and the multi-year investment programme, which are subsequently approved by the supervisory authority, which ensures their coherence with national and regional development plans.

7. Dissemination and promotion of the development plan and the multi-year programme.

- After taking into account the advice given by the relevant supervisory authority, the final version of the development plan and the multi-year investment programme are promoted and disseminated to technical and financial partners, both public, private, national and international.

- **Outcome of the stage:** Each local community is informed of the outcome of the two guidance and management documents as well as the achievements that concern them. Projects are developed and submitted to various sources of funding.

8. Implementation of MIP by annual segments.

- Each year the commune draws up an annual investment plan (AIP), which is the annual instalment of MIP and CDP. The commune's annual investment budget is the expression of AIP's financing needs. The annual investment plan covers the type of investment, costs, location, beneficiaries, and stakeholder participation in financing.

- **Outcome:** The commune has an annual investment budget, which is the result of the AIP.

9. Establishment of a monitoring and evaluation system for the development plan.

- The commune sets up information management and reporting tools to monitor the implementation of the annual instalment of the multi-year investment programme. These tools generate regular activity reports (quarterly). At the end of each year, these periodic reports are evaluated as part of a self-evaluation process of the commune's performance, which is initiated by the mayor. Self-evaluations are conducted mainly in these areas: (i) the functioning of the communal administration; (ii) financial resource management; and (iii) implementation of investments, and maintenance and operation of current infrastructure. Self-evaluation places particular emphasis on the strengths and weaknesses of the commune in each of these areas. The lessons learned are noted in the programme budget for the following year and in many cases result in capacity-building activities.

- Self-evaluation is part of the accountability process because the results must be shared with the local populations to inform them and raise their awareness on the overview of the commune's activities, responses to citizens' demands, and on the efforts that each individual must make in order to achieve the CDP objectives at the time of the overall review. The report on the self-evaluation is an annual opportunity for dialogue between communal institutions and their constituency.

- **Outcome of the stage:** Tools for reporting and capitalizing on the implementation of the development plan are set up and capacity-building measures applied with a view to their use. The report of AIP's track record is submitted to the local populations to assess the impact and results. It is presented in a public meeting to allow community representatives and civil society to take part in it.

3.1.3. Main lessons learned on local planning instruments

Lesson 1: *Shared knowledge of development problems and perspectives.* The beginning of mobilization of technical and financial partners to support the development plan is observed, which is starting to limit the dispersed, uncoordinated and uncooperative actions that preceded decentralization. With the development plan, locally elected officials have more knowledge and understanding of the territory, and therefore of the challenges of local development.

Lesson 2: *Local planning should be supported by better knowledge of the local economy.* The study of the commune's economic profile and opportunities should be done before or during the planning process and not after approval of the development plan. In other words, the diagnostic exercise and dialogue on the local economy is essential to give the CDP its true calling as an economic, social and cultural development plan.

Lesson 3: *Visibility of the CDP and monitoring of the commune's performance through the AIP.* One of the advantages of the AIP is to facilitate the monitoring of investments by financial partners who support communal investments and by the populations themselves. The AIP requires the communal institutions to streamline operational costs in order to free resources for the investment budget. The AIP thus becomes a powerful local tool in combating poverty, advocacy and social control of communal actions. At the same time, it allows the local populations to understand that it is in their interest to pay fees and taxes.

Lesson 4: *Weakness of inter-communal activities.* Little effort is made in the planning process to identify areas of comparative advantage in cooperation between communes in the UNCDF intervention areas. This can be explained by the extent of the internal problems that each local authority must deal with.

Lesson 5: *Lack of visibility of state sectoral policies.* The planning principles were generally handicapped by communal actors' lack of knowledge of sectoral policies. This is due to the fact that the decentralized services are often not well informed on the programmes of their own ministries. Despite the involvement of officials from these services in the commune's outlook analysis, their contribution is sometimes limited, which restrict the coherence of development plans with sectoral policies.

Lesson 6: *Unclear approval of plans by the supervisory authority.* It must be acknowledged that an analysis of coherence of the supervisory authority is not yet supported by a formal method of operation with precise tools. This situation leads to delays in approving communal plans. Consequently, approval is not given on a rational basis, to the extent that most intervention areas (departments, regions) do not have general outlines to serve as a point of reference to evaluate compliance by CDPs. The law is not clear on the minimum content of a plan. Furthermore, there is not always a reference plan to ensure conformity of local plans, to such a point that a synthesis of communal plans at the regional level within the framework of a blueprint for regional management would be a tedious exercise.

Lesson 7: *Participation is costly and takes time.* The main constraint to the participatory planning process is its repetitive nature. Numerous meetings are required to share information both vertically (territorial levels) and horizontally (meetings of specific groups or sectors). Although this approach leads to information ownership, strengthening of participatory democracy and construction of a development plan that reflects the real problems and demands of the people, it remains costly. For the moment, the communes cannot absorb such costs in their own budgets, which are generally small despite the progress made. The capacity of leaders of local organizations must be strengthened in order to take on the entire burden of leadership in the community so that there would be no need to turn to external donors at the local inter-community level.

Lesson 8: *Complexity of diagnostic and planning tools.* Given the low educational level of local actors and the rural population in general, it seems clear that unless the tools are simplified, in particular, the many interview questionnaires and voluminous documents drafted in French, it will be a difficult challenge for them to take over the planning process and its replicability.

Lesson 9: *The slow pace of implementation of state commitments.* Despite commitments made by state services, some funded infrastructure is still not operational due to a lack of supplementary investments or because staff has not been made available, for instance, in the fields of health or education.

Lesson 10: *Risk of raising people's expectations.* Participatory planning creates very high expectations that often cannot be met due to insufficient financial resources made available to the communities. This is a source of frustration both to the community and elected officials. Great care should be given to implementing this dynamic.

3.2. Participation mechanisms, frameworks for dialogue and arbitration procedures

Participation and responsibility are constants in the operating method of UNCDF projects in planning, activities, budgeting, implementation, and monitoring and evaluation.

The planning cycle described above shows how capacities of planning committees and commissions are established and strengthened at the commune level and within communes through village assemblies, thematic working groups, panels on women and youth, and with the involvement of providers and/or internal resource persons to facilitate dialogue. In all partner communes with UNCDF projects, the planning process has provided an opportunity for discussion with the local representatives of decentralized state services, technical and financial partners and local civil society. It has also fostered dialogue among all the authorities that form the community (locally elected officials, traditional chiefs, religious leaders, rural leaders). The participation mechanism has thus resulted in community technical workshops, bringing together elected and technical officials of the various sectors of economic and social life to further study the data collected in the diagnostic exercise and proposals from village and inter-village meetings. The planning documents, once adopted in the communal council, are then submitted to the supervisory authority, the chairman of the regional coordination and cooperation framework for development activities, who is in charge of verifying compliance with national and regional development orientations.

Three cooperation frameworks should be highlighted with regard to the institutional mechanism for operating the local development fund to enable the implementation of the commune's annual investment plans and support local communities' initiatives:

- **The tripartite review,** which is the forum for guidance and decision-making, is responsible for approving the annual work plan, harmonizing the local development tools tested and their development on the national level (see 2.3 for its composition). This body decides the level of local contribution to the LDF in order to adapt it to the context of the intervention area.

- **The steering and funds allocation committee** covers the entire intervention area. It is headed by the supervisory authority of the communes involved and includes mayors, some local representatives of decentralized state services, in particular finance (the Public Treasury), the development plan and the project support unit. This committee coordinates project activities in the field and monitors the observance of certain criteria for access to the LDF in the distribution of the annual allocation of this investment subsidy. The regulatory role of this committee is beneficial regarding the clear pressures on village communities, political pressures, and the risk of favouritism to win votes, which can influence fund allocation.

- **The local initiatives financing committee within** each commune is headed by the mayor or one of his deputies, and made up of representatives of economic groups, tax collection, the project support unit and the secretary-general of the mayor's office and/or the head of the financial affairs unit. This committee must select micro-projects that are not under the jurisdiction of the commune and finance them from the LDF. Mills, grain banks, agricultural and livestock supply banks, cattle and poultry and small business are examples of projects that, on the whole, produce the basics that: (i) feed the local economy directly, including the classrooms, wells, community health centres, etc; and (ii) help to improve the living conditions of the beneficiary groups. With a very high demand for financing by local organizations and limited funding availability, direct funding of local promoters by the commune might give rise to unmanageable conflicts, both among elected officials and between them and their communities. The available funds are disbursed in different ways each year as lines of credit or guarantee funds invested with micro-finance institutions, allocated to natural resource management activities, or for inter-commune cooperation according to the project.

3.3. Main lessons on participation mechanisms

Lesson 1: *Even though communal councils are composed of elected officials whose overall level is very disparate yet still rather low,* capacity-building activities have improved the team dynamic and have given all the parties involved an understanding of their role in the management of communal institutions.

Lesson 2: *The functioning of coordination frameworks presents real problems in large-scale communes* because of isolation, distance and travel costs to attend meetings.

Lesson 3: *Financing of activities of local initiatives is challenged by the inability to meet the demand for financing IGAs,* the lack of competent local micro-finance institutions, the risk of non-payment linked to a lack of expertise in high-growth sectors and sponsors' low management capacity levels. The decision to allocate part of this financing to natural resources management or to inter-communal activities in certain intervention areas is a last resort, because monetary poverty is a serious threat to natural resources management, and finding innovative ways to combat it effectively, despite the risks of non-payment, remains a challenge in poverty eradication today.

Lesson 4: *Lack of will among local elected officials to play a primary or significant role in providing subsidies to local economic initiatives because of the risk of favouritism that this assumes.*

3.4. Instruments for financing and local development

3.4.1. *Local development funds and their characteristics*

LDF objectives

The local development fund (LDF) is a financial instrument for supporting the budgets of partner communes with UNCDF projects for financing public, social, collective and economic investments in development and poverty eradication in rural areas. These are global subsidies (financing equipment) intended to stimulate performance of local governments and IVLUC, to promote institutional development and help to build capacities of local actors to enable them to carry out the micro-projects identified and conceived at the local level.

Determining the size of LDF

The size of the overall LDF allocation is based approximately on population size, geographic considerations (distance and isolation) and a base amount per capita, which applies to all communes in an intervention area. In addition to these criteria, some UNCDF projects have instituted a system of additional rebates at a preferential rate or discounts based on efforts to mobilize local resources (Benin).

Resources are allocated to each commune on the basis of a financing matrix establishing the financial commitment of each party (commune, population, State, development partners, etc.).

Conditions of LDF eligibility

A commune's eligibility for LDF is based on legal and regulatory as well as financial conditions. The following conditions are part of a gradual and sequential approach. Their degree of application also depends on the motivation of locally elected officials, the mayor in particular, and the country's socio-political context.

Basic conditions for all projects

- Prior signing of a partnership agreement and a co-financing agreement for LDF between the commune and the UNCDF project;
- Having a communal development plan and a multi-year investment plan drafted according to a participatory approach and adopted by the communal council with a record of the deliberations and a letter of approval by the supervisory authority (auditor's certificate);
- Objects of financing related to the jurisdiction of communes or rural local social and professional organizations, which are compatible with poverty eradication;
- Limited environmental impact.

Conditions specific to some projects
are infrequently applied due to administrative inertia

- A significant proportion of projects from local initiatives benefiting women's groups;
- Establishment of an outline for steering the annual activities of the commune development plan;
- Availability of core technical staff, including the secretary-general and the tax collector, for the implementation of administrative, financial and accounting procedures;
- Observance of school and health cards and availability of staff for posts;
- Adoption and implementation of a management programme for the maintenance of community housing;
- Protocols of agreement with social and professional organizations for the management of infrastructure when applicable, in view of the provisions in effect;

- Adoption and implementation of a policy for access to information, especially by the local populations;
- A register of the minutes of communal assemblies and publication of the communal council's decisions;
- The commune's operating budget established in advance for the current fiscal year: obligation of a local counterpart included in the commune budget with clear identification of funding sources;
- Performance criteria regarding mobilization of local resources and in terms of physical and financial implementation of the previous allocation;
- At least two-thirds of the actions included in the co-financing agreement for the AIP for the current year completed and provisionally delivered;
- Respect for the proportion of LDF allocations on the basis of geographic and demographic criteria observed, and facilities defined;
- Contributions of communes collected at the source, directly by the General or Regional Office of the Treasury, and public accounting of the budget subsidies granted to them by the State.

Funds and financing sectors under LDF

The LDF of UNCDF projects are usually structured by three facilities: (i) *a social and collective investment fund* for construction, repair or rehabilitation of collective social infrastructure; (ii) *an inter-communal fund* or a fund focused on natural resources management allocated for cooperation projects between the project's partner communes and relating to management of shared natural resources, environmental protection and infrastructure of interest to all communes (rural roads); (iii) *a support subsidy for local economic initiatives* aimed at supporting IGAs and combating monetary poverty.

The three funds are part of the communal budget for direct support. Further, the subsidy to local economic initiatives is allocated in some cases by the commune to a financial institution following an agreement either in the form of a line of credit and/or loan guarantee funds to the benefit of local economic promoters or directly managed by the council.

With the implementation of decentralization in the sub-region, LDF experiences implementation in real time of a model of budget transfer to the communes based on programmed use, transparent allocation and rapid disbursement through the Public Treasury circuit (Benin and Senegal), by the channel of investment and development agencies (ANICT in Mali), directly into bank accounts in the name of local governments (Guinea), or managed by project teams since there are no communes and financial institutions (Niger and Burkina Faso).

Transferred LDF resources are recorded and accounted for in communal budgets. They aim to finance the investment priorities of each of the communes as defined in the participatory planning and budgeting documents. The share of resources allocated to each sector depends on the resources that can be mobilized and the order of priority of projects included in each AIP, as illustrated below:

Benin: ADECOI 2004

- Infrastructure and equipment: education (51%), merchant equipment (21%), health (12%), transport and communications (7%), water and sanitation (5%), agriculture and livestock farming (2%), environment (2%).

Mali: PACR-T, 2003

- Infrastructure and equipment: agricultural sector (29.7%), water (19.4%), education (14.5%) and livestock farming sub-sector (12%).

This distribution of LDF is generally in line with the concerns and priorities defined in the development programmes of the communes concerned, and fully observes the UNCDF guidelines. Where there are national mechanisms for funding local governments, as in Mali with ANICT, UNCDF avoids creating parallel mechanisms of allocating investment funds to communes.

LDP investment financing and the disbursement system

The process involves the following steps for each investment: (i) recording the commune contribution in the financing plan; (ii) registering the commune contribution in the commune budget; (iii) mobilizing counterpart funds by the Treasury by keeping a part of funds transferred by the central government; (iv) mobilizing counterpart funds by the Public Treasury; (v) recording in the commune budget and implementation by the commune.

The system of financial programming and mobilization mentioned above includes the system of funds transfer from the country's Public Treasury, which implies that UNCDF should make the necessary funds available to the Treasury on the basis of the decision of the steering and funding allocation committees. The funds are then transferred into a special account in the Treasury, opened in the Public Treasury records at the central or regional level (see 1.4.5 and annex 2).

Local co-financing systems

During the pre-decentralization phase, community contributions were made by a private collection of funds from individuals and rural organizations based on a list of contributing households or organizations in each village. With decentralization and the advent of communes, contributions come or should mainly come from commune budgets based on fees, taxes and levies. The local co-financing system therefore involves the commune both as beneficiary and project manager.

The financial participation in the LDF, which is based on the communal budget, breaks with traditional practices of financing development based on contributions and voluntary subscriptions of the population. These informal practices present problems of resource mobilization and transparent management. Moreover, these subscriptions do not permit the commune to levy local taxes to increase its contribution to the formal LDF mechanism.

3.4.2. Financial arrangements for resource mobilization

**Towards communal programme budgets
for a coherence of actions in local development activities**

UNCDF supporting projects contrast with traditional practices of turnkey implementation of investments that have infringed upon — since the advent of decentralization — the communes' area of authority. The originality of the UNCDF project approach in the financing mechanism of local development projects is based on the following factors:

- *Determining funding of communes:* The demographic criterion has always been taken into account in determining the funding granted to communes, in all funding types. Mali has added a geographical coefficient to favour the most isolated communes where costs of the approach considerably impact on the cost of realizing investments.

- *Evaluating the performance of communes:* The commune's performance is evaluated at the end of each year. The results of this evaluation have a positive or negative impact on the funding of communes, according to whether the communes perform well or not. This is to promote an evaluative culture and the duty to achieve a given result so that support mobilized for the implementation of CDPs would truly contribute to improving the living conditions of the poor and not on increasing property spending of the communal councils.

- *The principle of budgetary support:* funding allocated to communes come under the heading of budget investments. Funds are disbursed through the use of the services of the Public Treasury (in most countries) and occasionally through a national agency for financing local authorities. In all cases, the financing agreement with communes does not target specific micro-projects; it is more of a global grant for supporting communal investments. It is up to the communal council, therefore, to distribute the funding according to its investment priorities. The advantage is that harmonization and transparency are encouraged in the partners' financial contribution. This is because the procedure of drawing up, adopting and approving the commune budget facilitates the allocation of resources and monitoring of the participation of various partners in local development. The results are:

- better accountability of elected officials and strengthening of their credibility with the citizens whom they represent;
- simplified recording of accounting of investments in commune capital;
- an opportunity to build capacities of elected officials and local public administrations in understanding public finance procedures;
- better absorption capacity for investment funds;
- more comprehensive and less piecemeal implementation of development plans
- control of financial flows coming from various partners, making it possible to coordinate and monitor development activities and stimulate a more balanced and harmonious approach to land use management in the commune.

- *The use of the Treasury circuit is a double-edged sword:* This can actually help to develop the state instruments and at the same time, be a source of major delays. In the French-speaking system, with the principle of *unicité de caisse*, (single cashier) the state services are essential. In using the circuit of disbursement through the Public Treasury, it is up to these services, not the project, to prove their effectiveness and efficiency. Success in this area is varied. In Senegal, for example, the period of time for the transfers between the central State and the communes has been reduced by five months; in Benin, the State's financial difficulties caused major problems in making these funds available, and due to the low level of human resources in the Treasury services at the local level, entrepreneurs could not be paid within a reasonable time.

- *Co-financing of investments:* financial subsidies granted to communes can be disbursed in investment co-financing with other sources of financing.

- *Contribution in cash:* In most of the projects, preference is given to local contribution in cash formerly registered in the local budget. They have often served to pay start-up costs to enterprises in order to make the commune responsible for managing financial flows, but also to hold local enterprises responsible for malfunctioning.

Mobilization of investment funds by communes has proven to be very important. This can essentially be explained by the principle of budget support and the simplification of public contracting procedures for local authorities. In carrying out investments, the communes' financial participation has exceeded expectations in many cases, although there is more to be done in local resources mobilization.

The external resources mobilization for investment has proved highly useful. In many cases, the LDF, used as a counterpart fund, has served as a lever to raise other external financing. This leverage effect is particularly strong in Mali with ANICT and in Senegal with EU funding in UNCDF areas.

In the countries as a whole, the communes' financial participation varies from 5% to 25% according to the type of investment. This threshold depends on the level of monetary poverty and ecological vulnerability of each intervention area.

Finally, the level of local taxes recovery influences the funding granted to communes. As a rebound effect, this has had repercussions on the villages and subdivisions, reflected in the tax collection rate as a criterion for evaluating funding requests. A local community with an unsatisfactory level of tax payment can therefore lose funding for its infrastructure to the advantage of another that is up to date with its tax payments. The direct consequence of this practice has been a net improvement in collection of communal taxes.

3.5. Local Contract Cycles

Calls for competitive bids and awarding of contracts by the commune are done in compliance with public contracting laws in each State. The mayor awards the contracts on the recommendations of the commune's bid evaluation commission headed by one of the deputy mayors, which also includes members of the communal council, experts and the tax collector. In general, agreements on public bids and awarding of contracts for industrial and commercial services are submitted for approval to the supervisory authority. However, deadlines for approving these contracts are provided by law in order to avoid delays that could affect AIP implementation.

Prescribing this method of awarding contracts aims at leading the communes gradually to set up a bidding process that is transparent and in compliance with the state code for public tenders. The steps followed were:

- *The institutional level:* (i) drafting a manual for contracting, which is carried out by communes; (ii) providing training (analysis of bids, awarding of contracts, etc.); and (iii) supporting communes in establishing the commune committee for bid analysis and evaluation.

- *The level of management of the contracting cycle:* (i) preparing requests for bids; (ii) launching the bid submission process either through announcements, limited consultation or open bid requests to the market segments authorized by the country's laws; (iii) opening bids and evaluating proposals; (iv) the mayor's signing of a letter of notification of the decision; (v) signing the contract between the mayor and the service provider or vendor with a service order indicating the date of project for beginning project implementation; (vi) monitoring project implementation by the commune, the local communities, the consulting engineering firms, the project management unit and the competent state services; (vii) submitting a report on the prior use of funds before making a new funding request; (viii) signing a notice of receipt on the completion of any activity financed by the beneficiary (commune, village or inter-village community or community group), the lender and the project; (ix) setting up a management committee or recruiting a manager to ensure the operation, maintenance and sustainability of the infrastructure; and (x) conducting a year-end community self-evaluation of the AIP to evaluate the impact of the infrastructure as a whole through an analysis of services rendered to the populations and their maintenance.

3.6. Development of local project management and expertise

Community project management and the principle of budgetary support provide that all bidding procedures for contracting contracts must be done at the commune level. In contrast to traditional interventions where construction, delivery of equipment and services provision are centralized in the project management unit, in this case, each commune carries out the investment procedures. Time is saved compared to the centralized model for interventions where the works are handed over ready-made for beneficiaries.

The development of local project management requires building the capacities of locally elected officials and commune staff in regard to competences of communal institutions, local planning, contracting, set-up of micro-projects, construction management, local governance, decentralization and communal administration. Additional capacity building concerns drafting and executing of the communal budget, managing of municipal budgets, the archives, administrative reviews and the gender aspect, etc.

The capacity-building strategy was based on procedures in effect in each country and experience gained through support to communes at the preliminary phase.

The results obtained in terms of improved work skills are notable. Nevertheless, the assets remain precarious because of the professional instability of communal workers (older, with low educational levels) and the high turnover rate among communal councillors when their terms of office end. Mali has suffered particularly in this area.

The emergence or consolidation of formal local companies for public works and buildings remains an important benefit from the support provided by UNCDF projects to communes. The transformation of jobbers in the intervention area into formal companies is part of the strategy of tax enrolment for these economic operators, who then begin to pay taxes to the commune.

Training of locally elected officials, commune staff and the LDF mobilization facility has generally had a positive impact. Communes, groups, village and inter-village committees have demonstrated expertise of the development tools initiated by UNCDF projects.

3.7. Quality and functionality of built infrastructure

The building of infrastructure uses the available educational and health facilities chart and water points. In general, the commune respects the norms and standards in effect and involves the state technical services, which must monitor their observance. The projects also help the communes to recruit business advisers to provide more detailed technical monitoring of work sites until final delivery. In villages with VLUC or IVLUC experience, there is social know-how in monitoring work sites, which requires jobbers to follow the procedures in the work plan, in particular regarding measurements and quality of materials, etc.

Payment of entrepreneurs is graded and based on evaluation questionnaires on the level of accomplishing the assigned tasks (daily reports) compared to disbursements (deductions) at each stage of the timeline of the work until the final handover, which can take place several months after the infrastructure has been in use. The problems detected are rectified by the entrepreneur prior to the final handover.

It must be recognized that capacity building provided by projects for the benefit of workers, masons in particular, has led to a clear improvement in the infrastructure quality. Despite these efforts, it is clear that communes that do not have a technical service, and most do not, are naturally less capable of monitoring work sites, which causes problems.

One of the major difficulties is the lack of quality materials and the isolation of sites where infrastructure is to be built. In some cases, the problems in providing supervision and monitoring are compounded by work that does not follow regulations.

The strategy for maintaining and upkeeping infrastructure is an essential dimension of the impact of the infrastructure on living conditions in the community. Efforts at upkeep are variable and communes generally lack the appropriate budgetary resources. The following shared observations have been noted:

- *infrastructure for common use,* such as town halls: its maintenance can easily be seen as part of the commune budget;
- *infrastructure for non-commercial community use:* its maintenance is provided by the beneficiary community through a management committee that reports to the communal authority. On the other hand, communities that have not had VLUC experience and where there is not this tradition, face serious problems regarding the responsibility for maintaining community infrastructure;
- *market infrastructure:* most often, it is offered without charge to economic interest groups to manage, or a manager is hired. Most management contracts concern shops or stalls in markets. Maintenance of this infrastructure is provided by IEGs and specified in the management contract.

Most of projects have not been able to come to an agreement with the communes that could lead to a policy on communal facilities management. Management committees have not always been established according to the rules spelled out in the agreements with communes before the financing starts. They are often set up after or while the work is being carried out.

Comparative analysis on local infrastructure delivery

Infrastructure built within the framework of UNCDF projects is of better quality than similar infrastructure observed in the intervention areas. This is certainly a logical result of giving responsibility to the beneficiary community and the commune, which assures the project management. It is also a result of the remarkable effort in capacity building of local jobbers and all the administrative support given to them in order that they become formalized and gain more markets, thus allowing them to continue to improve their skills. In addition, the leadership process and the administrative and financial processes that govern the definition of needs until they are met constitute determining factors in the quality and functionality of the infrastructure. Technical monitoring provided by various actors (experts, elected officials, project management units and the population) can be added to this. However, particular attention has not been given to the comparative costs of the projects in terms of investments by NGOs, sectoral ministries and delegated project management (executing agencies for highly labour-intensive projects).

3.8. Capacity building and handover and sustainability strategies

The various cooperation and dialogue forums created or strengthened at the commune, inter-commune and supra-communal level are organizational and administrative assets that assist in the decentralization process in the six countries. They provide opportunities for exchange of information, advice and mutual learning, which enables local actors to share experiences in managing their communes, and when possible, strategies for maintaining and renewing investments. Supervisory bodies, such as school parent associations, management committees and users' associations, are some of the local strategies to provide good management and to render UNCDF project outcomes sustainable. In addition, a major network of locally elected officials, state agents, NGOs, and both women and men has been trained through this form of public management, gradually forming a significant body of local actors that could assume leadership in the local development process.

Similarly, individuals trained in negotiation skills have acquired the ability to discuss their projects with technical and financial partners. Eventually, these local actors will be able to attract supplementary external financing to fuel the local economy. Moreover, the development by communes for rental services on commercial and non-commercial facilities is part of a strategy of follow-up and sustainability of efforts to combat poverty by increasing their capacity to contribute to the commune budget.

Finally, an important toolbox has been set up for all projects, which represents precious capital for continued capacity building among local and even national actors. It includes: (i) a guide for designing a local development plan; (ii) a guide for designing income-generating micro-projects; (iii) a manual for presenting and managing the LDF, (iv) a guide for contracting; (v) a manual for drafting a budget; (vi) a collection of laws and regulations on legal aspects of operations; and (vii) various reports on relevant studies on economic potential and flows.

3.9. Strategies to promote local economies

Promotion of the local economy is part of an approach to rendering sustainable the achievements of the UNCDF projects' support to communes, which is essential to combat the monetary poverty that affects efforts to eradicate poverty in all other sectors. The commune's ability to meet its investment costs in a sustainable manner in order to improve local living conditions depends on the amount of money available to its inhabitants. The goal here is to help generate wealth so that the poor have income and purchasing power that will improve local circulation of money and hence their access to basic social services.

In sum, the promotion of the local economy is a strategic sector for the communes' viability and at the same time, it is a job that requires know-how and specific knowledge of local economic potential and limitations. For the time being, it is still the weak link in the chain of support to local governments. In fact, it is about to or will be tested. This is the reason that all UNCDF projects have supported communes in conducting studies of their local economies, which have resulted in greater awareness of economic potential, evaluation of strengths and weaknesses of the economy and in analysis differentiated by commercial sector. In certain areas, these studies have already led to identifying each economic sector's contribution. This knowledge of the local economic structure will be pursued in the medium term through institutional partnerships to improve information on markets—price, seasonal price variations and variations in products availability in the commune, the area and the country—in order to make better use of opportunities in the flow of local products.

In addition to these new directions, projects are providing increasingly less direct financing to economic actors for their rotation funds. However, market infrastructure for collective use comes under the jurisdiction of the commune, and minor infrastructure that could belong to groups (warehouses, grain banks, manufacturing equipment) is financed by the LDF. Funding needs of IGAs are supported through decentralized financial systems where a credit and/or guarantee fund is established.

3.10. Main lessons learned on financial and contracting mechanisms

Lesson 1: *Completeness of the information on every step in the process is a pre-condition for laying the foundation of a culture of transparency.* One of the best practices acquired from the LDF is promoting and tracing the financial contribution of the population in carrying out public investment.

Lesson 2: *an LDF aligned with national financial procedures.* Alignment of communes' financing with national public finance procedures has proven effective when the country does not experience pressure from the Treasury. The prejudice that the Public Treasury and its principle of *unicité de caisse* (single cashier) are inefficient and unfavourable in managing the funds of local authorities has proven invalid. It results in greater credibility of the State and public treasuries in the sub-region. This experimentation has shown that public procedures are viable in remitting project funds and monitoring their implementation. The effectiveness of the system clearly depends on the quality of human resources.

Lesson 3: *an original system of financial support focused on budget support to communes.* The originality of the financial support system is based on taking into account the evaluation of performance in allocating funding, the principle of budget support and the possibility of co-financing of investments with other partners intervening through budget support. The funding agreement with the communes does not target specific micro-projects, but rather represents a global subsidy intended to support communal investments in line with the UNCDF mission. Thus, it is up to each communal council to distribute the funding according to its investment priorities outlined in the AIP, originating from the multi-year investment programme and the communal development plan.

Lesson 4: *a financing system with a leverage effect.* Experience shows that it is extremely difficult for a commune in a rural area to come up with contribution at different rates from one programme to another through its own resources. Co-financing with a leverage effect have often led to the development of a financing investment system perfectly in line with the local authorities' capabilities.

The implementation of the co-financing system by the communes and the UNCDF project have demonstrated the possibility of: (i) mobilizing the sum of contribution of the commune and of the State; (ii) disbursing the contribution of the commune and the State more quickly than in the past; (iii) avoiding work stoppages due to inability to mobilize contribution; and (iv) including investment expenditures in the commune budget and ensuring that the communes manage them.

Lesson 5: *positive impacts in the budget process and management of communal services.* **Many advances have been made:** (i) regular meetings of the commune held with acceptable frequency; (ii) preparation of AIP and annual budgets by almost all communes in the intervention areas within the legal deadlines and of acceptable technical quality; (iii) in many cases, controlling procedures for public contracting; and (iv) clear improvement in the management of public records, in particular, shorter delays in providing clients with records.

Lesson 6: *positive impacts but an inadequate political will.* In general, elected officials are concerned with ensuring that the communal institutions provide accessible and effective services to the people. This awareness is laudable, but major efforts are still needed by elected officials, populations and the government to strengthen the means of communal institutions. For the moment, the transfer of state resources to local governments is weak and local investment programmes still depend on international aid.

Lesson 7: *significant efforts still needed to promote local governance.* In the absence of a durable strategy to continue building capacities of newly elected officials, there is reason to fear that the quality of local governance will deteriorate. Activities to inform and train local communities should therefore be strengthened in order to create a pool of community leaders that would emerge in the communal councils over the years to come. Better still, considering that the decentralization and communalization process are in their infancy, more ambitious national capacity-building programmes for decentralization should be considered over the long term.

Lesson 8: *weak linkages at the territorial level of decentralized financial systems and the banking network.* The financial facility for implementing the LDF faces several constraints: (i) an inadequate banking network that does not facilitate liquidation of payment orders for service providers and vendors; (ii) lack of human and material resources of the local services of the Treasury, sometimes causing delays in processing payment requests; and (iii) lack of credible structures for micro-finance in many communes, which limits the promotion of supporting subsidies for local economic initiatives through the LDF, and which results in a low level of utilization of this fund for some projects. The problem with funding is still the lack of true national micro-finance policies in these countries, which hinders the implementation of solvency strategies of the poor and the improvement of their access to financial services within their own context.

4] CONTRIBUTION TO THE MILLENNIUM DEVELOPMENT GOALS (MDGS)

4.1. MDGs and poverty reduction strategies in West Africa

On 8 September 2000, the United Nations General Assembly adopted the *Millennium Declaration*, which put forward a vision of a world free of extreme poverty by 2015. This Declaration consists of eight *Millennium Development Goals* (MDGs), with 18 targets and 48 indicators. Each country is subsequently adapting these global objectives to national poverty issues.

With the cooperation of the United Nations system, each of the UNCDF countries of intervention has already adjusted its MDGs. More than just a series of indicators, the MDGs is a monitoring and accountability system for mobilization at the international, national and local level as well as in each development initiative to confront the poverty affecting many people in the world (see the table below).

Table 3: Links between MDG and Proverty Reduction Strategies (PRS) in project countries

MDG	2015 Target	Conclusions of national reports
Goal 1: Eradicate extreme poverty and hunger	Target 1: Reduce by half, from 1990 to 2015, the proportion of people living on less than a dollar a day. Target 2: Reduce by half, from 1990 to 2015, the proportion of people who suffer from hunger.	The changes in indicators studied do not leave much hope to reduce by half, the number of persons living below the poverty threshold or suffering from malnutrition by 2015.
Goal 2: Achieve universal primary education	Target 3: Ensure that by 2015, children everywhere, boys and girls alike, will be able to complete a full course of primary schooling.	The goal "universal primary education" by 2015 could be reached, but efforts should be supported by all to improve quality of education and ensure children complete the first course of primary schooling, as well as reduce the disparities between girls and boys.
Goal 3: Promote gender equality and empower women	Target 4: Eliminate gender disparity in primary and secondary education, preferably by 2005, and at all levels of education by 2015.	Changes in indicators predict reaching this target by 2015, but not in all countries. This target is still strongly influenced by socio-cultural inertia and will show but weak progress by 2015 if education in the rural areas is not adequately strengthened.
Goal 4: Reduce child mortality	Target 5: Reduce by two thirds the mortality rate among children under five.	The countries are still far from achieving this target. The current trends of infant and child mortality rates do not leave room for optimism. It is necessary that governments expend great effort in this regard.
Goal 5: Improve maternal health	Target 6: Reduce by three quarters, between 1990 and 2015, the maternal mortality ratio.	Efforts in reproductive health by governments in the subregion, with the support of development partners, allow hope that the target could be reached.

MDG	Target by 2015	Conclusions of national reports
Goal 6: Combat HIV and AIDS, malaria and other diseases	Target 7: Have halted by 2015 and have begun to reverse the spread of HIV/AIDS Target 8: Have halted by 2015 and begun to reverse the spread of malaria and other major diseases.	The strengthening of actions to combat AIDS, facilitation of access to antiretroviral (ARV) treatment and the promising outlook for developing a forthcoming, widely distributed vaccine against AIDS could give rise to hope for the stabilization and possible reversal of the trend towards 2015.
Goal 7: Ensure environmental sustainability	Target 9: Integrate the principles of sustainable development into country policies and programmes, and reverse loss of environmental resources Target 10: Halve by 2015 the proportion of people without sustainable access to safe drinking water. Target 11: Achieve by 2020 a significant improvement in the lives of at least 100 million slum dwellers.	The observation of indicators shows that the trend of losing natural resources will be difficult to reverse despite many initiatives undertaken in sustainable development, and particularly, the taking into account of the environment in poverty reduction strategy documents. If the trend shown by the implementation of different projects and programmes were maintained, in 2015 some countries could hope to achieve or even go beyond this goal of sustainable access to drinking water. Nevertheless, this achievement is not certain in the Sahelian and desert regions. In general, the policies and programmes undertaken in order to access a decent living environment will hardly be up to the challenge due to costs of construction materials, the enormity of needs in social housing and the great needs in sanitation and public hygiene.
Goal 8: Develop a global partnership for development	Target 14: Address the particular needs of the least developed countries	These debt reduction programmes are implemented and will allow to increase available resources for the poverty-reduction strategy.

The MDGs in West Africa are based on some of the following major problems: (i) the low level of development of IGAs and the lack of infrastructure in communities, which leads to growing monetary poverty and food insecurity; (ii) problems with land related to pressure from exploitation and intra- and inter-community conflicts causing displacement of people and animals; (iii) environmental degradation (drought, floods, erosion, deforestation, decline in soil fertility, overgrazing, pollution); (iv) the isolation of some areas affecting mobility of persons and goods, in particular access to markets and public services; (v) lack of facilities and difficulty in access to safe drinking water and primary health care; (vi) the spread of infection and sexually transmitted diseases such as HIV/AIDS; (vii) illiteracy and school drop-out; (viii) lack of capacity building among the local populations for good governance of public affairs and the increasing pace of participatory democracy; and (ix) inequality towards and violence against women and other vulnerable groups, as well as socio-cultural burdens detrimental to the promotion of human rights.

At the institutional level, decentralization and sectoral public policy form the backdrop for drafting and implementing poverty reduction initiatives. The features of political will expressed in these poverty reduction strategy frameworks and documents place great importance on harmonious land use management, creation of wealth, development of human resources, promotion of the private sector, national solidarity and respect for human rights. From this viewpoint, the main lines of action in these documents are: (i) sustained economic growth, job and income creation; (ii) development of the production sector; (iii) development of basic social services; (iv) promotion of good governance, capacity building of human and institutional resources and decentralization; and (v) protection of the environment and sustainable management of natural resources.

The conclusions on the countries' possibilities of achieving the MDGs by 2015 when considering the degree of achievement of these goals indicate some rather hesitant trends due to lack of sufficient resources and the slow pace of decentralization and deconcentration in the six countries. Unfortunately, most of the MDG indicators are not disaggregated to the local level, which is, however, a prerequisite for integrating MDGs into territorial planning. The difficulty lies in the lack of testing of a methodology that would make the MDGs effective in managing local governments since their primary aim is to combat poverty and promote local development.

4.2. Hearing the voices of the poor and disadvantaged in their choices on local investments and services to offer

Support forums for social mobilization to listen to the poor

In order to strengthen the role of local communities in the local development process, UNCDF-initiated support programmes have favoured as a principle of intervention: (i) creation and/or consolidation of forums for coordination, dialogue, arbitration and advocacy at various structural levels in the intervention areas; (ii) creation and/or promotion of village and inter-village development committees as well as community project management committees; (iii) the establishment of partnership mechanisms to monitor projects and participatory studies/surveys/evaluations to measure the populations' satisfaction with how the support suits their expressed needs. Including UNCDF programmes in the decentralization dynamic brings about systematic support to community management of construction projects by strengthening capacities of communal and rural councils to practice the skills and responsibilities entrusted to them by their national laws. Due to their legitimacy through elections, local officials represent an important element of the voices of the poor, which is strengthened by the direct support given to various networks of local actors who have other types of legitimacy in their communities: women's groups, groups of producers, livestock farmers, artisans and village development committees.

The voice of the poor is polyphonic and heard at various levels of the territorial structure and in several sectors of economic and social life. In each intervention area and partner local government, this voice has been raised in the implementation of the local planning component, which has mobilized various segments of the local community, independent of their ethnicity, gender or social position. All the marginalized groups (lower castes), persons disadvantaged by gender and age (women and youth), and villages marginalized for various reasons (historical, cultural, political) have been involved in the development of the process. The various workshops, meetings and forums held by the heads of village, inter-village and commune-level consultation framework have allowed choices to be made that meet the local populations' real needs.

Difficulty in arbitrating among the voices of the poor and disadvantaged

The voices of the poor naturally express their experiences and hopes. But the needs—all important and sometimes very urgent—are greatly varied, while the mobilized local resources are still very weak and additional resources are limited relative to the severity of the situation of poverty. Major problems then arise in making decisions during the land use planning process and establishing the timetable when arbitration on priorities to be programmed for each community is not based on a concept of complementarity and solidarity among communities.

The participatory approach in a planning process should take proper time so that the poor may be able to discuss among themselves and their elected officials, and take into account the characteristic strengths, weaknesses and opportunities of each community. This effort thus requires mediation, which should be based on *good documentation* (production statistics, demographic profile, economic and ecological potential, schools, health care centres, number of clean water points, risk exposure factors) to support the analysis by the local populations. This is the reason that *the voice of the poor* is supported, for expert advice by the voice of *resource persons*, who share the daily life of the populations. Despite the connection between the two types of voices, the populations' expression may not always take into consideration the means for solving their problems of poverty in the short and medium term. This is often what leads to plans that — despite being highly participatory and taking into account the voice of the poor — do not produce results of the magnitude required. UNCDF's approach has therefore made partnership systematic, which leads to mutual or complementary means for synergistic activities that demonstrate the maxim, "we are stronger together than alone."

The voice of the poor is necessary for good local governance and achievement of the MDGs

The voice of the poor is a sign of transparency in local governance, a condition for commitment on the part of the poor and marginalized to the work of developing their community and for raising their civic awareness. From this ability to express themselves, and the opportunity offered by decentralization to be recognized as full-fledged actors, they will in turn accept their duty to pay taxes, having understood the relationship between paying taxes, the development plan and the poverty reduction strategy that leads to solving their problems.

In UNCDF's experience, this style of governance has led to the promotion of an open and inclusive approach towards the poor and marginalized, which has allowed the interests of all actors present and all social classes in the community to be taken into account in local planning. The organization of common spaces and the composition of structures set up transcend all traditional divisions (social and especially political affiliation, place of residence, etc.) and consider the interests of all the groups involved. This inclusive approach sometimes corrects the lack of representation on communal councils.

Finally, the nature and functionality of the investments produced are indicators of the voice of the poor, because they express the consideration of their needs. The voice of the poor helps to limit the failure of development projects; i.e. the achievement of the MDGs depends on the roles and responsibilities of the poor in the process of developing their community.

4.3. Choice of the location of investments

Carefully determine relevant locations for the success of spatial planning

The decision on where to invest is an element of the planning process, especially spatial planning. In practice, UNCDF support to decentralization and local development must distinguish among several relevant locations to place investment projects.

Investments at the community level cover (i) infrastructure and equipment for the entire village community or area (village, town and subdivision together); and (ii) infrastructure and equipment for supporting a specific organization within the village community, such as women's groups devoted to certain IGAs and livestock farmer groups.

Investments at the level above the community are found (i) at the intermediate level between the commune and the village or area; and (ii) in commune capitals that are often the most urbanized areas of the territory or the rural community and which cover a number of neighbourhoods in a town.

Investments in institutional capacity building of the municipal administration that concern the mayor's office and branch offices of administrations at the intra-community level only. These investments, which are aimed at modernizing administrative, technical and financial management, are meant to provide clients, particularly the poor, with quality services within a reasonable time and at a price that they can pay. These investments mainly cover computerization of services, electrification, telephone systems, the civil registry, the archives, the means of transport and the equipment for sanitation infrastructure (road, rail and waterworks network).

Some criteria to develop in a participatory space planning process

The choice of locations for investments leads to many difficulties in the planning process. There are villages that demand infrastructure due to bearing a significant portion of the rural tax payments or simply due to historical factors. Some village chiefs with political influence also attempt to legitimize the choice of locating facilities in their areas in order to retain or gain favour with voters. This is also the case for central villages that want to continue to polarize the rest of the villages because of their historical or religious role or their administrative advantages. In the face of all these obstacles, care must be taken that the choice of the location meets some objective criteria that will allow progress towards the MDGs. In addition to practical criteria (LDF arbitration rules) in UNCDF projects and programmes, the following should be considered in order to streamline the process of identifying an appropriate location for each type of investment at the planning stage:

At the sociological and institutional level:
- the voice of the poor and marginalized;
- the voice of elected officials and local development leaders;
- the voice of all social classes.

At the technical level:
- the size of the population;
- the concept of the central village with its satellite towns and communities;
- geographical accessibility;
- environmental constraints and the status of natural resources that affects food security and community health;
- schools and health care centres;
- availability of safe drinking water points;
- the level of mobilization of tax resources (taxes and local levies): poverty should not be a pretext for failure to promote a culture of taxation, which is an essential condition for sustainable local development, and which justifies it as a criterion for allocating local development funds;
- specific constraints on women in developing their IGAs;
- budgets predefined at the territorial level of local government: for example, the AECOI programme decided that at least 60% of financing for the annual investment plans would go to *arrondissements* outside the main town in the commune. This formula established in the procedural manual is targeted solely at the interests of the poor and is fully in keeping with a perspective of harmonious and balanced management of the communal territory.

Local planning, when it relies on the voice of the poor, enables social cohesion to be maintained and restores the citizenship of Individuals often given little consideration or marginalized. The mere fact that the poor feel that they are taken into account because their voices are heard creates in them the need for openness and learning, engaging them in a process of change that they themselves embody.

4.4. Frame of reference to measure impact and effects

Concern over impact to combat poverty effectively

Impact is understood here as all the capacities acquired and developed from the investments in infrastructure and equipment, as well as technical and investments in building technical and organization capacities of local authorities, local communities and local development workers. For programmes supporting decentralization and local development, the impact — the aim of the investments — mainly concerns poverty reduction through assisting populations in enjoying better living conditions in their daily lives.

To measure an impact, an observation mechanism must be set up to trace facts on the ground (production) and behaviours (reactions) that inform and show the acquired capacities.

The impact may involve the internal governance of local governments; the quality of relationships among support partners; the quality of utilization of mobilized resources; and initiatives to strengthen financial autonomy regarding the operating costs of those authorities. The impact of a project is also measured by its functionality, which in turn is verified through maintenance operations of its water points, classrooms, health centres, mills, market warehouses and purification ducts, etc. The impact is also the voluntary periodic restocking of grain in food banks to cope during lean periods in order to limit price surges in the village and cases of child malnutrition.

In order to be able to evaluate changes in living conditions, the local populations and communal administration have to get used to tracing these impacts and the problems encountered in a rational manner. This impact tracking system has often helped to provide a more reliable basis for annual reports of communal councils and the annual programmes, which provide an opportunity to update the local development plans.

The monitoring and evaluation components in each UNCDF programme include two modules:

- A module on *monitoring implementation,* which is focused on analysing differences between what was planned and what was actually carried out, including the completion rate on the physical and financial levels, and factors explaining the gaps observed and problems encountered.
- A module on *monitoring impacts*, which is focused on measuring the changes in the situation and behaviours of direct and indirect beneficiaries, including an array of indicators supplied with data from surveys and studies, or information given at meetings or general assemblies of the local populations, locally elected officials and institutional support partners.

Measurement tools

In the two monitoring modules, major consideration is given to respecting the competences devolved to the local governments according to the law of the country, the national poverty reduction strategy paper, communal councils' records of deliberation, and working documents from the various committees for investment management. The minutes of committees to allocate LDF together with the procedural manual are important tools in evaluating the soundness of practices for allocating investment funds. In addition to these tools, many others are highly useful to the MDGs because they allow measuring effectiveness, efficiency, sustainability, replicability, or are used as a model of investments regarding the improvement of living conditions for the poor and local governance. There are essentially three types of tools: (i) the communal development plan, annual investment plans, and work plans covering several months; (ii) activity reports, financial reports, and training reports; (iii) programme orientation and monitoring committee reports, external evaluation reports, and audit reports.

Limits of the monitoring of impacts according to MDG criteria and indicators

In order to harmonize the monitoring system with the MDGs at the national level, the monitoring of indicators of local development plans must be based on the MDG model. Unfortunately, none of the countries has broken down the MDGs at the local level to support the impact of local development plans. In sum, as long as the UNCDF intervention areas lack a regional and local scheme linked to the national MDGs, it will be difficult to effectively measure the contribution of supporting activities to poverty reduction in the disadvantaged communities of these areas. One of the weaknesses in making the MDGs work is the lack of a functioning internal monitoring and evaluation mechanism at the local governments' level to support the implementation of local development plans. This can be explained by several constraints: limited access to information technology and electricity, scarcity of qualified staff; and the cost of data collection and processing.

To reverse this trend and to enable appropriation of the MDGs in communal management, the following actions should be carried out:

- supporting local authorities in establishing reliable, regularly updated databases linked with national MDGs;
- rendering the monitoring system on the MDGs more accessible in all the programme intervention areas;
- sharing the system with other partners;

- consolidating achievements in archiving strategic documents of the local government;
- building capacities of local governments in planning and programming/budgeting of annual investments.

The analysis of programme and project financing to support decentralization and local development thus shows that they take into account the multidimensional nature of poverty in their design and implementation, as summarized in table 4.

Table 4: Linkage of UNCDF programmes and projects with the MDGs

MDG referred to	Profile of UNDP/UNCDF investment programmes and projects
Goal 1: Eliminate extreme poverty	1. Strengthening of technical and institutional capacity of local actors (VLUC, IVLUC) communes, local associations, decentralized services, local NGOs, local labour); 2. Advocacy of principles of good governance in basic social sectors and promotion of the local econom;y 3. Establishment of a local development fund in support to the IVLUC and communes to carry out investment programmes, including a guarantee fund to support IGAs; 4. Management of irrigation areas; 5. Promotion of market gardening; 6. Grain banks; 7. Warehouses for products; 8. Sheltered mills; 9. Cattle vaccination areas, and slaughterhouses / veterinary pharmacy; 10. Commercial equipment; 11. Promotion of traditional or improved energy sources; 12. Rural roads and tracks, and road building works;
Goal 2: Provide primary education for all	13. Classrooms and equipment; 14. Meeting and training rooms for adults; 15. Housing for teachers;
Goal 3: Promote gender equality and the advancement of women	16. Social mobilization for girls' schooling; 17. Production inputs to relieve women's burden of labour; 18. Promotion of women in village and inter-village development committees; 19. Centres for reading, literacy and training;

MDG referred to	Profile of UNDP/UNCDF investment programmes and projects
Goal 4 : Reduce infant mortality	20. Community health centres;
	21. Health care posts;
Goal 5 : Improve maternal health	22. Maternity centres;
	23. Pharmacy depots;
Goal 6 : Combat HIV/AIDS, malaria and other diseases	24. Ambulance motorbikes;
	25. Medical kits;
	26. Training for matrons and care-givers;
Goal 7 : Ensure environmental sustainability	27. Village wells, drilled wells and water pipe networks;
	28. Latrines;
	29. Forest management, quickset hedges and training in techniques for planting, pasture management and forage crops;
	30. Soil regeneration and conservation.

The following matrix supplements tables 3 and 4 to show in which way local development objectives harmonize with the MDGs to structure the development plan of the local governments and help to combat poverty.

Table 5: Sample planning table for local development aligned with the MDGs

Local development objectives	Implementation activities	MDGs and targets	Costs ('000 of FCFA)	Execution period (years)				
				1	2	3	4	5
1. Improve food security	1.1 Agricultural water resource management	MDG 1 – target 2	150,000		▓	▓	▓	
	1.2 Soil regeneration and conservation	MDG 1 – targets 2 and 11	200,000	▓	▓	▓	▓	▓
	1.3 Grain bank	MDG 1 – target 2	80,000	▓	▓			
....								
....								

See table 3 for the MDGs and their targets.

4.5. Impact of support programmes in the field

Improving the situation of the poor means,
above all, supporting a local development plan

Local development plans have become real tools that have raised interest both from the communities themselves and support partners. The fact that UNCDF chose rural areas and their poverty pockets as priority intervention areas is significant. Improving rural areas means giving rural people a chance to thrive in their own environment, and not to risk it is to cause many of these poor to move to the city and abroad. The problems caused by emigration are in part due to insufficient investment in rural areas. The choice of strengthening available infrastructure and equipment in health care, education, water supply, land reclamation and the local economy (commercial equipment, processing equipment, guarantee funds for productive credits, etc.) can only benefit the people involved: more pupils, both boys and girls, enrolled in school; more support for teachers; better understanding the challenges in local development; improved management of local public affairs; increased capacity for advocacy and lobbying by local organizations; and fewer problems of morbidity and mortality, including a decline in HIV/AIDS prevalence (see MDG 2, 3, 4, 5 and 6).

All the village and inter-village committees that were formed through the planning and project management process constitute a critical mass of local actors (men and women), who actively participate in the leadership of local community life — politically, economically and socio-culturally (see MDG 3).

In all the countries of the sub-region, the missions of decentralization, the communal centres, development agencies and the communes themselves are greatly inspired by the approach to local development management. They have been promoted in particular through local planning, and village and inter-village development committees under support projects. This promotion of achievements is a major focus of the partnership approach that characterizes the interventions in support of UNCDF-initiated local development (see MDG 1 and 8).

Combating rural poverty means stabilizing
family farms and feeding the poor

The many activities promoted in the areas of agriculture, livestock breeding, soil restoration, the environment, forestry, pastoral water supply and small irrigated plots have served as a basis for expanding the production base, thus creating the conditions for true food security and combating diseases related to malnutrition in children (see MDG 1, 6, 7 and 8).

No local development is sustainable without the mobilization of local resources

Investments in commercial equipment have allowed for the restructuring of markets, making them cleaner and safer, the setting up of management committees, and above all, to allow women to better carry out their IGAs to combat monetary poverty (see MDG 1). Fees collection for market stalls and rentals of boutiques and shop to users in most beneficiary communes have promoted a significant and rapid increase in local tax resources in the general interest of the populations, the poor in particular. This emerging taxation culture is an asset for sustainable development by allowing the communes to maintain their investments in operational condition and to make investments out of their own funds. Many communes therefore gradually contribute to the local development fund even if the levels of mobilization are highly variable and need improvement.

Dynamics for mobilizating local resources

In Mali, for example, several communes have established a rule of arbitration among their respective communities that takes into account the tax and levy recovery rate in the funding allocation. A village or subdivision that has not paid its taxes in full will therefore have lower priority than another that has. Financial participation by communes in sharing costs of creating investments thus becomes an essential condition for continuing efforts to combat poverty even beyond the support period for the development partners.

4.6. Lesson learned and improvements needed to achieve the MDGs

The conclusions of national reports on the progress made towards achieving the MDGs have shown that without sustained effort through increased resources for investment in the social and commercial sectors, it will be difficult to achieve the MDG targets by 2015 even though significant progress is expected in the education and water sectors. Local public investment contributes to the recognition of the MDGs, but could contribute more. The MDGs must still be brought to the attention of local actors to ensure that they will be given more attention in local planning.

Lesson 1: *The portfolio of actions promoted in support programmes is multidimensional* and takes into account the complexities of poverty. It includes: (i) the set up of socio-communal and commercial collective infrastructure and equipment; (ii) natural resources management and environmental protection; (iii) strengthening of local governance and results-based management; (iv) a participatory approach and a gender perspective; (v) links between all levels of the commune's territorial structure; (vi) consideration of all sectors of economic, social and cultural life that impact on poverty reduction; and (vii) mobilization, strengthening and development of local skills.

Lesson 2: *Support programmes strengthen community project management while reinforcing local communities.* Investments are inconceivable without multi-year planning, annual programming, delegation of responsibility to communal authorities, the local development fund, and the financial contribution of the commune.

Lesson 3: *Taking the MDGs to the local level is required to strengthen monitoring of local development plans.* While the nature of investments and their mode of implementation fit in perfectly with the MDGs, none of the programmes discussed in this study and none of the intervention areas are monitored or evaluated on the basis of MDG targets by 2015. This situation represents a bias at the level of local governments' management that must be corrected by adapting the MDGs to the local level so that they can be sustained by the support programmes. On this issue, it would be appropriate to make the communes responsible since their principle mission is to combat poverty.

Lesson 4: *It is absolutely necessary to take the MDGs into account in updating local development plans.* The integration of the MDGs into local development plans and annual investment plans results in a results-based programme budget. This will be beneficial for the performance evaluation of each commune and decentralized State services. However, it assumes the implementation of a deconcentration policy and the transfer of competences and resources that are still held by the ministerial departments.

Lesson 5: *There is a need to consider local and regional development plans in sectoral planning at the central level* to ensure greater coherence between local and national policy. The coordination of territorial policies with sectoral policies remains a challenge to be addressed in each of the States of the sub-region.

5] Partnerships established

In the implementation of support programmes for decentralized local development in West Africa, UNCDF and its project teams seek to build national, local and international partnerships. More than a necessity, for UNDP/UNCDF, partnership is a key component of its strategy for combating poverty and achieving the MDGs.

5.1. The challenges and winning formulas for partnership

A partnership is a contract of objectives, which may be formalized or not. As an instrument for mobilizing the stakeholders involved in pursuing the common goal of implementing a shared project, its importance lies in the common understanding that poverty is multi-dimensional, complex, very costly to eradicate, and very demanding in terms of the solutions to be applied. In this sense, the notion of partnership, which is inherent in UNCDF programmes, means that all stakeholders concerned with a territory and the living conditions of its people must be convinced of the need for cooperation and for mutual assistance in the combat against poverty.

5.1.1. What are the challenges in a partnership?

Achieving more and better results together than alone

The main objective of decentralization and local development is to mobilize local actors and their partners in tackling the problems of local populations and their territories through better local governance, which capitalizes on local potential and provides adequate responses to development challenges. The advantage of this approach is that it provides the partners with mutual knowledge, establishes or strengthens technical and economic complementarities, and implements new forms of development-based solidarity. UNCDF's support therefore aims at contributing at the organizational, technical and financial levels, as well as with equipment to allow for the creation of development centres by exploiting social and economic potential. Satellite settlements will develop around these centres so that local land use plans may be able to encourage sustainable and harmonious local development. Such a challenge can be met only in partnership.

Why the need for partnerships in local development?

Partnerships enables: (i) synergy and coherence of actions; (ii) development of the comparative advantages of each stakeholder; (iii) leverage to increase investments and ensure their more fair and harmonious distribution; (iv) pooling of expertise and financial resources for the benefit of all projects; (v) each partner to learn from the other; (vi) harmonization of approaches; (vii) mitigation of leadership conflicts between donors; (viii) better local governance with greater transparency at all levels as well as more active social monitoring; (ix) the requirement for accountability to be more easily accepted by elected officials; (x) relatively less limiting support of the populations' acceptance in efforts to mobilize local resources through taxes because they see and benefit from the fruits of the partnership; and (xi) improvement in the level of local workers' skills.

Indeed, when the project areas are as extensive and as remote as those in which UNCDF intervenes, it is generally understood that no development programme by itself can have sufficient resources to support all of the communities living in these areas. Only the establishment of a solid partnership with various stakeholders can ensure the successful implementation of the projects to be undertaken. Partnerships have often been established with NGOs on the ground to achieve this objective. UNCDF has relied on such collaboration to reach the poorest sectors and to ensure that the devolvement by communities' of their responsibilities — in terms of village and inter-village land-use committees' activities — is better monitored. This experience, carried out with NGOs CARE and the French Association of Volunteers for Progress (AFVP), has resulted in remarkable development work in northern Mali.

5.1.2. What are the winning formulas for a partnership?

In order to be successful, a partnership must comply with a number of principles that the parties must integrate into their joint approaches towards a shared goal. This schematic outline is based on and patterned after instruments and analyses set out in the country reports.

The winning formulas for partnerships drawn from lessons learned in UNCDF programmes in West Africa can be summarized in nine key principles, which form the basis of a partnership charter for decentralized local development for the MDGs.

- **Principle 1: A formula for partnership in the basic cooperation documents**. Project documents, funding agreements and procedure manuals must clearly allow for all forms of beneficial partnerships at the institutional and operational levels for a support programme for decentralized local development.

- **Principle 2: Integration of proposed programmes and projects into national policies.** Bringing the projects in line with the MDGs and the country's decentralization policy is essential since the State is the principal guarantor of national land use policy.

- **Principle 3: A common vision of partnership**. This vision is the great dream of success in reducing poverty and achieving decentralized local development, whose realization requires individual, collective and institutional commitment.

- **Principle 4: Linkages between the institutional structure of the partnership and the institutions and competencies of local authorities.** The partnership must seek to strengthen the capacities of communal institutions in order to enable them to improve the quality of management of local public affairs.

- **Principle 5: Local planning focused on local democratization**. The partnership must provide coherent responses adapted to the populations' needs and not on what the donors and technical partners consider to be beneficial to them. The relationship with the local populations must be substantiated by an approach characterized by participation and accountability at all phases of the project cycle. This participation requires the mobilization of local resources, specifically, the promotion of a local tax culture, by the payment of fees and taxes that would allow to maintain and renew socio-collective investments.

- **Principle 6: Synergy and mutually reinforcing actions**. The partnership must seek a leverage effect and coherence in the total support for local development as well as a balanced distribution. This approach must promote the integration of remote communities and marginalized groups, particularly women, into the process of land transformation so that local governments could become a true space of solidarity. This partnership also requires cooperation between neighbouring local governments (inter-communality, for example).

- **Principle 7: Flexibility on the part of the different stakeholders.** Each partner must show understanding and rrespect for the other within the limits of his or her prerogatives.

- **Principle 8: Transparency in the implementation of common projects and close attention to each partner's image**: communications, monitoring of meetings, joint visits to field operations, and full traceability of the actions of each stakeholder are ongoing efforts needed to strengthen and further develop cooperation.

- **Principle 9: Development and sound management of local potential**: essential conditions for local communities' sustainable access to the dynamic of change in their living conditions offered by partnerships are: the strengthening and development of local workers' capacities; development of natural potential and comparative advantages at the institutional level; and of the geographic, sociological, cultural and economic situation.

5.2. Forms of partnership

The search for financial support or collaboration towards a common development objective in line with the strategy to combat poverty can therefore take several forms, which are characterized here on the basis of UNCDF experiences.

5.2.1. Institutional and operational partnerships

The willingness to cooperate is shown at two strategic levels: institutional and operational.

Institutional partnership: This type of partnership is based on the similarity of projects at the national level, which is the reason that actors are concerned with their consistency and capacity for mutual reinforcement. The actors therefore create a melting pot of exchange, a kind of thematic or sub-sectoral coalition. This is the case of the coalition for natural resources management projects in Burkina Faso, which has provided support for the National Plan to Combat Desertification (PNLCD), of which the UNCDF country projects are a part. The PNLCD has become: (i) a genuine forum for harmonizing methods of intervention in the different projects; (ii) a forum for advocacy to lift the constraints to cooperation, in particular, the bureaucratic burden of the public administration; and (iii) a framework for mutual sharing of experiences at the national level, which gives it greater visibility. This type of partnership is much more effective at mobilizing decision-makers, financial partners, management committee members of projects, and project heads. The institutional partnership operates mainly at the strategic level and is therefore concerned with questions of approach, procedures, relations with the government and donors. It provides the intra- and inter-sectoral links at the national level as well as management of the relations inherent in international partnerships.

Operational partnership: This type of partnership aims at mutual reinforcement between the actors involved in the same intervention area and providing the same services to local governments and their populations. The geographic similarity is but one determining factor since collaboration can extend to exchanges of experiences and goods and services between actors. These actors may not share the same territory but be involved in the same area of activity and concerned with solutions to specific problems arising in the field, especially those affecting the populations. Different partnership agreements may involve the same actor, with each partner representing a different focus of interest. For example, UNCDF programmes are in a differentiated partnership with FAO's Special Programme on Food Security (PSSA) for the regeneration of soils and for accessing fertilizers. At the same time, however, they have established a differentiated partnership with World Food Programme to support the initial allotment of grain banks. With other NGOs, cooperation concerns a finance research programme to support the implementation of local development plans prepared by inter-village land use management committees. At the same time, the international partnership provides training for the officials in these committees.

5.2.2. Methods of formalizing a partnership

A partnership may or may not be formalized, but it should be formalized as a show of commitment. A partnership may be formalized in the project document and the financing agreement that specifies the project's institutional framework.

At the operational level, the process of formalizing the partnership may begin with: (i) the geographic location of the support actors operating in the field; (ii) a list of potential donors and lenders; and (iii) relations with neighbouring communes. This formalization is done by the signing of contracts, agreements and charters, among others. It operates with different social structures of local populations for implementing and managing selected activities under the local development plan, such as municipal offices, land use management village committees, parent-teachers associations, management committees for health centres and water supply points, etc.

Failure to formalize or institutionalize a partnership may be due to a partnership of circumstance, or one created on an ad hoc basis or for a specific action. This type of partnership, based on a verbal commitment, is often semi-formalized, through mission reports of project managers submitted to the communities, illustrated or not by audio or audiovisual aids and photographs.

5.3. Actors in partnerships

The partnership dynamic is not only a coalition of donors or public administrators, but it is also a purposeful and participatory approach open to other types of actors.

Partnerships assume the capacity to go beyond the traditional considerations of leadership and to break down the different barriers created between actors. When opting for inclusion and integration (as opposed to exclusion, marginalization, antagonism and ignorance or the failure to recognize the capacities of others) partnerships create functional ties among actors and bring them closer together. But what types of actors?

Irrespective of the form chosen, partnerships involve various categories of actors depending on the interest created by the intervention area and actors' motivation in building partnerships.

On principle, the actors or future stakeholders are only partners insofar as their will and commitment to the struggle with which the future associated partner stakeholders identify. Alternatively, the partner status is determined by the third principle, namely, the shared vision. More specifically, actors can be individuals, institutions, associations or enterprise. A partnership may group together: (i) *at the national level:* central and decentralized public administrations, local governments, development agencies, civil society organizations, the private sector, local communities; and (ii) *at the international level:* structures or individuals representing bilateral or multilateral cooperation agencies, international solidarity organizations, and foreign territorial authorities.

5.4. Areas of partnership

The areas of partnership are determined by the missions of each party, the competences of the local governments and the needs of the local communities.

Without being exhaustive, the areas of partnerships observed within the framework of UNCDF programmes in West Africa are as follows:

At the institutional level

- Strengthening the local governance capacities of local elected officials and civil society organizations;
- Technical and/or financial assistance for implementing the annual investment plans of local governments and inter-village and village land use management committees;
- Advocacy (dialogue on national and local public policies);

- Participatory local planning and harmonization of supporting tools for local development (guide to local planning, indicators of local governance, criteria for access to local development funds);
- Communal committee for the selection of local micro-projects;
- Support for the mobilization of resources by promoting contacts between land use management organizations and economic groups, particularly women, with micro-financing institutions with or without the set-up of a guarantee fund at the institutions by UNCDF;
- Joint or complementary activities for building infrastructure and installing equipment. For example, UNCDF builds modular classrooms and latrines, one of the partners provides electricity and water, and another provides the tables and benches, while others provide training for the parent teachers association and for the school administrators in order to ensure effective management;
- Comprehensive monitoring (the project management committee and local committee for the monitoring of local development projects);
- Capitalization of experiences and exchange of know-how.

At the operational level
- Food security: grain banks, input banks;
- Strengthening of technical capacities in specific areas of activity;
- Exchange visits;
- Natural resources management: protection and restoration of soils, and reforestation;
- Social and community health and sanitation, water supply, school and educational facilities and commercial infrastructure and equipment.

5.5. Steps in the establishment of a partnership

The establishment of a partnership requires several phases, summarized in six key steps in Table 6.

Table 6: Cycle for setting up a partnership

Steps	Actions	Results
1	Preliminary contacts for information to trigger the will to cooperate through the exchange of documents concerning activities or projects of each negotiating partner with the option to visit projects.	Adhering to the idea of creating a partnership dynamic. The common vision identified.
2	Development of a draft memorandum of understanding, a charter or agreement, detailing: • Centres of interest in collaboration, particularly, the partnership principles; • The common goals pursued • Commitments of each partner; • The implementation mechanisms and procedures of the collaboration and the partnership • The frameworks for collaboration, harmonization and ensuring coherence of interventions within the partnership framework • The common strategies of conflict prevention and management; • The methods of monitoring the memorandum of understanding, the charter or the agreement	Collection of centres of interest proposals. The proposals are discussed and a draft memorandum of understanding/charter/agreement is produced.
3	Finalization of the memorandum of understanding/charter/agreement	The draft formalized partnership received a no-objection notice from all stakeholders.
4	Signing of the partnership agreement	The agreement enters into force.
5	Connecting the offer of each stakeholder with the development plan of the local authority	A compilation is drafted of the shared offer within the framework of the partnership.
6	Monitoring of the implementation	Periodic meetings to keep apprised of the implementation and to revitalize the partnership.

5.6. Partnership Outcomes

The outcomes of the partnership must be assessed in terms of the value added. Partnerships have clearly created synergies for many projects, allowing for coherent and coordinated responses to questions related to: (i) food security; (ii) the functionality of school establishments, adult learning centres and health centres; (iii) water supply for populations and cattle; (iv) market infrastructure and equipment that help to lighten the burden of IGAs; (v) loans for productive activities to combat monetary poverty; and (vi) activities to protect and restore soils and village plantations.

Partnerships have achieved the following results, among others:

- an increase in the level of investments of local development funds;
- reduction in dispersed and uncoordinated actions through strengthening local supervision, giving more responsibility to communal councils for managing development projects in their localities;
- greater visibility of available investment capacities that can be mobilized for the intervention area by strategic sector in the combat against poverty;
- the consolidation of budget support mechanisms through better demonstration of the possibilities of using state financing to effectively manage project funds (the national budget, financial control and the Public Treasury);;
- eliminated or reduced competition in the search for financing through joint projects with shared responsibility that give coherence to the relations between financing sources that have fewer small projects within their portfolios;
- common ground in the procedures for managing support to communities: procedures that are less contradictory and less focused on a system of competition between development projects;
- mutual learning experiences;
- issuing of joint implementation reports, thereby limiting the proliferation of contradictory technical and financial reports and promoting a results-driven reporting system that is not exclusively focused on the source and object of financing.

The examples below show the relevance, effectiveness and impact of partnerships in combating poverty:

- A partnership with the Senegalese rural electrification agency made it possible to electrify school and health equipment, thus resulting in a marked improvement in the populations' comfort. The health centres that benefited from this partnership will be better able to conserve medications and handle emergencies, even at night.
- UNCDF is providing guarantee funding to microfinance institutions to enable groups to access loans from them. This is the case in the partnership between UNCDF and the Mutual Credit in Kaffine, or the FADEC in Kébémer, Senegal.

The promotion of a dynamic of partnership based on the mobilization of several forms of bilateral and multilateral cooperation contributes to achieving MDG 8, *Develop a global partnership for development.*

The outline below shows the introduction of a local partnership and of a shared intervention area in an international partnership. It shows how this partnership tackles the problem of extreme poverty and hunger through food security by working on local communities' productive and management capacities, fertility management and agricultural land protection.

Figure 1: Example of the strategic framework for merging action in a UNCDF-initiated partnership for MDG 1

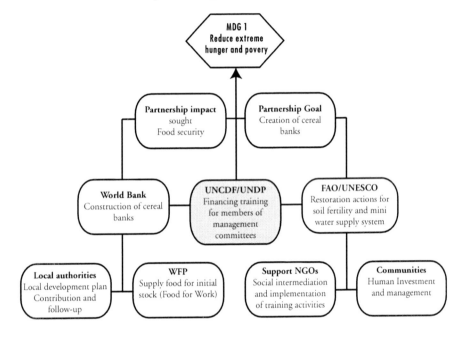

5.7. Risks and pitfalls to avoid

The risks of a partnership for decentralized local development are at several levels, particularly at the time of implementation and/or during partnership growth. These risks and pitfalls are determined by the socio-political and institutional context of the country, the system of public land management in the intervention area and the commitment of the actors.

The main risks and pitfalls identified within the framework of UNCDF projects are occasionally poor preparation of partnerships, insufficient involvement of the decentralized state services, lack of flexibility, the difficulty of reaching consensus on the schedule of meetings, the difficulty of harmonizing administrative procedures among donors, and cumbersome payment procedures.

Poor preparation of the partnership

A partnership is not a forced marriage, but it is a demanding process (see principles above). In areas with a heavy concentration of development partners and civil society organizations, it is not easy to create a partnership by mobilizing all institutional actors. It is absolutely necessary from the outset to make a selection in order to base the partnership on credible actors who are respected in the intervention area. A map analysing the various actors in the intervention area using the strengths, weaknesses, opportunities, threats (SWOT) approach is essential, and would include: (i) analysis of the strengths and weaknesses of the partner in relation to its areas of action; (ii) analysis of the actor's opportunities for the partnership; and (iii) analysis of the threats to the partnership if the actor's reputation evokes a negative image or dubious suspicions in the local environment.

Insufficient involvement of the decentralized state services

Although these services are permanent and aim to supplement the assistance and advisory services provided by projects, their involvement in implementing these decentralized local development projects is limited. The gap in terms of financial, technical and material resources between the project structures and these decentralized services is so great that it creates frustrations or even jealousy that can go so far as leading to a refusal to participate in the partnership. Impaired by a power struggle that is far from constructive, the results of the projects enjoy limited capitalization and development after the completion of their cycle. To avoid this regrettable situation, the practical procedures of the partnership with public administrations should be clarified as soon as each project is formulated. The poor quality of these services is due not only to the situation of poverty, but also to the lack of an effective deconcentration policy to assist decentralization and the poverty reduction strategy.

Lack of flexibility

To engage in a partnership is to submit to a group discipline regardless of the scale of the resources provided by each stakeholder. A partnership may limit a part of the stakeholders' freedom by the social control exercised by each partner. Such control should be seen as a common desire that the partnership succeeds and not influence each partnership stakeholder's performance.

Occasional difficulty in reaching consensus in scheduling meetings

Functional constraints may occasionally arise, especially where the scheduling of meetings is concerned, or when some partners do not find the solidarity or mutual support that they expected when embarking on the partnership. Quite simply, certain partners may repeatedly ignore the contents of the protocol or agreement.

Difficulty in harmonizing the administrative procedures of donors

The procedures of each partner may constitute a limiting factor, despite the will to cooperate, quite simply because the project document did not leave the necessary room to allow the project team to engage fully in the partnership dynamic. The issue of project supervision can also divide partners. Certain projects are based on strict respect for joint supervision, while others, such as World Bank projects, prefer communal supervision delegated to the local authorities for building infrastructure within the community's jurisdiction.

Cumbersome payment procedures

The failure of the Public Treasury to pay the invoices of service providers and suppliers on time, and the bureaucratic delays in issuing cheques by the financial services of the municipality weaken the partnership. For example, economic operators may be reluctant to continue the work or to pre-finance them, which affects the scheduling of activities and creates payment difficulties for certain partners.

5.8. Main lessons learned on the progress and issues of partnerships

Lesson 1: *Strength through unity* and local partnership is an essential condition to ensure harmonious and sustainable development of local governments.

Lesson 2: *The local development plan is a tool for bringing together* partners and their actions to combat poverty. It channels opportunities for resolving populations' problems and avoids duplication and waste of energy and resources.

Lesson 3: *A partnership is not a forced marriage but a voluntary approach* that nevertheless has constraints. Group discipline is the key to its success, and exemplary conduct by each party determines its credibility and effectiveness.

Some general considerations concerning the UNCDF intervention framework are as follows:

- Since UNCDF's philosophy of intervention is based on intervention on demand, it would seem logical that lessons learned from this capitalization should be highlighted in the project documents. Their content and procedure should be reviewed to better reflect the risks and pitfalls associated with partnerships;
- Project formulation should better integrate the determination of the reference situation, particularly with regard to the MDGs;

- The post descriptions of teams in the field are often ill-suited to the results or strategies of intervention. (PADMIR, for example, has no officials in charge of monitoring and evaluation, nor any communication specialists.);

- Current procedures of centralized accounting and financial management are, in several respects, inadequate for implementing projects supporting decentralization and local development.

6] Conclusion

UNCDF is aware that the combat against poverty is a process that requires time and methodologies, but also the means to profoundly and sustainably improve the living conditions of the poor. Decentralization is an essential condition for achieving this goal, tackling poverty and laying the groundwork for local development.

Decentralization should be the means to integrate marginalized groups, minorities and women in the decision-making process so that they can fully enjoy their citizenship. In addressing this challenge of social justice, UNCDF and its partners supported local governments in exercising their legal authority. Clearly, UNCDF is not starting from zero and the lessons learned from previous projects serve as a basis to improve its intervention methods on various government levels: the commune as a channel of support; local communities serve as the main focus of its efforts to reduce poverty; and the provincial, regional and national levels act as important counterparts for strengthening partnership and sharing experiences for the benefit of the communes.

In the local planning process, the LDF, strengthening of local development management capacities and good local governance remain the common threads in UNCDF's mission to promote local development. Over the past five years, different, new initiatives have been undertaken or old projects extended according to the countries of intervention.

In order to promote a greater understanding of its various instruments of intervention and their impacts, UNCDF has chosen to draw on lessons learned from its projects in West Africa, which are summarized by this document. The main element to consider is that these UNCDF projects follow the financial procedures of the partner States and their anchorage in communal budgets/programmes in the form of decentralized budgetary assistance. The agreements for implementing these projects were prescribed and were successful in mobilizing local resources as an effective strategy for community project management and an indispensable condition for the sustainability of the implemented infrastructure. They have effectively generated a number of very interesting impacts:

Impacts on local governance, land-use planning and environmental governance:

- Introduction of equity, justice and transparency in the contracting process, which is a good indication of good local governance;

- Expansion of dialogue forums among various decision-making centres at the local level;

- Promotion of a dynamic for commune's performance evaluation;

- Dialogue between the communes of each intervention area, gradually preparing the way for genuine inter-communal cooperation to enable the mutual sharing of resources for joint actions or shared services;

- Promotion of technical approaches for the management of natural resources by the DRS, forested village land, management of grazing areas.

Social impacts

- Emergence of a dynamic for promoting local development that succeeded first in gaining people's trust, then motivating them to action through capacity-building, planning and implementation of development projects, mobilization of local resources, and evaluation of the communes' performance;

- Access to basic social services (health, education, village water supply, cereal banks, etc.);

- Taking into consideration of the specific interests of women and reducing their daily tasks, thereby creating the conditions for their full participation in the management of local affairs;

- Integration of marginalized groups into the social dialogue on local development by strengthening their participation in the management of local affairs (management committees, parent teacher associations, communal commissions, village land use committees, and inter-village land use committees);

- Conflict prevention linked to the exploitation of shared natural resources by promoting integrated and sustainable resources management.

Financial and economic impacts

- Leverage effect to attract funding from other partners;

- Increase in the populations' purchasing power through the financing of IGAs;

- Creation of income-generating employment and sources to increase consumption demand and therefore supply of services;
- Improvement in the productive base, an essential means for increasing production and thereby improving food security;
- Improvement in the mobilization of local resources;
- Strengthening of the financial capacities of local governments.

Although these impacts are consistent with the MDGs, it must be recognized, nevertheless, that there are certain weaknesses: (i) in certain cases, lack of national decentralization and deconcentration policies or of implementing legislation for the laws on decentralization to support the achievement of the MDGs, and the complete transfer of power to the communes; (ii) the limited number of development guidelines at the national and regional levels for analysing the coherence of communal development plans; (iii) lack of adequate linkages between micro-finance structures and the banking network, which affect the development initiatives of local economies; and (iv) inadequate human resources in communal institutions.

The consolidation of the impacts of the UNCDF projects will depend greatly on the political will in the countries of intervention, efforts to tirelessly pursue the MDGs, and on strengthening the operational resources of local governments, as well as forums for dialogue between local actors. But there is room for hope in the enthusiasm created by decentralization among the populations and locally elected officials.

BIBLIOGRAPHY

GNIMADI (Aime). Capitalization of the experiences of projects for the support of local development and decentralization in West Africa: the case of Benin (Capitalisation des expériences des projets d'appui en développement local et décentralisation en Afrique de l'Ouest : Le cas du Bénin), UNCDF, November 2005.

OUTTARA (Oula, Claude). Capitalization of the experiences of projects for the support of local development and decentralization in West Africa: the case of Burkina Faso (Capitalisation des expériences des projets d'appui en développement local et décentralisation en Afrique de l'Ouest : Le cas du Burkina Faso), UNCDF, November 2005.

BAH (Mamadou, Lamine). Capitalization of the experiences of projects for the support of local development and decentralization in West Africa: the case of Guinea (Capitalisation des expériences des projets d'appui en développement local et décentralisation en Afrique de l'Ouest : Le cas de la Guinée), UNCDF, November 2005.

ONGOIBA (Hamidou) Capitalization of the experiences of projects for the support of local development and decentralization in West Africa: the case of Mali (Capitalisation des expériences des projets d'appui en développement local et décentralisation en Afrique de l'Ouest : Le cas du Mali), UNCDF, December 2005.

HALIDOU (Saidou). Capitalization of the experiences of projects for the support of local development and decentralization in West Africa: the case of Niger (Capitalisation des expériences des projets d'appui en développement local et décentralisation en Afrique de l'Ouest : Le cas du Niger), UNCDF, November 2005.

DIOUF (Papa, Babacar). Capitalization of the experiences of projects for the support of local development and decentralization in West Africa: the case of Senegal (Capitalisation des expériences des projets d'appui en développement local et décentralisation en Afrique de l'Ouest : Le cas du Sénégal), UNCDF, November 2005.

ANNEX 1: CHOICE OF CRITERIA AND INDICATORS FOR EVALUATING PERFORMANCE OF LOCAL GOVERNMENTS

The performance criteria of the local governments regarding each of the areas/instruments for implementing their projects have been approved by the Management and Disbursement Committee during the course of a workshop.

Source: ADECOI: *Évaluation de la performance des communes du projet ADECOI : suivi des acteurs au titre de l'année 2004, Bénin* (Evaluation of Performance of Communes in the ADECOI Project: Monitoring of Actors in 2004.)

Note: A certain weight (relative importance) has been attributed to each of the criteria by the participants in the *Comité d'orientation du projet et d'allocation financière* (COPAF, Project and Financial Allocation Steering Committee) workshop. It was noted that the weight attributed to each of the criteria would remain the same throughout the life of the project and would be used for calculating the performance of communes in partnership with ADECOI.

Table 7: Criteria and indicators of communal performance assessment

Domains/tools	Criteria	Indicators
Local governance	Holding of regular communal council sessions	• Number of regular and extraordinary sessions with deliberations • Method of convocation used to to allow participation of the population (radio, posting, individual convocations)
	Principle of legality: decisions taken come out deliberations	• Percentage of the mayor's decisions having been previously debated within the communal council
	Information sessions organized to inform citizens	• Number of restitution sessions • Posting • Broadcast radio debates
	Citizens consulted on the quality of services	• Number of opinion polls per year • Number of debates (radio, public)

Domains/tools	Criteria	Indicators
Local planning	Annual Investment Plan (AIP) in line with the Communal Development Plan (CDP)	• Percentage of investment projects that originate from CDP • Percentage of realisation with respect to AIP
	AIP promoting partnership within the villages as well as inter-communality	• Percentage of investments made in the rural *arrondissements*
	Monitoring-evaluation mechanisms set up to follow-up on CDP and AIP are efficient	• Existence of an annual report on the AIP • The existence of a minutes of quarterly council meetings of local collaboration and coordination • Organized restitution meetings
Local finances	Increase in own revenues of the commune by at least 5%	• Rate of increase of own revenues of the commune between 2003 and 2004
	Respect of legal deadlines for adopting preliminary budget	• Dates of consultations with local population
Local development fund	At least 60% of investments realized outside the capital	• Percentage of LDF invested in the rural *arrondissements* • The entire local counterpart funding was allocated within the deadline given
	Allocations for operation and maintenance set up and used	
Contracting	Procedures of contracting respected	• Date of launching the call for tenders (CFTs) • Date of opening of the CFTs • Date of assessing the CFTs • Date of market notification • Time period between the notification and signing of the contract
	Disbursement on the basis of documentary evidence and monitoring reports of the work site	• Time period between the payment request and the disbursement
Gender aspect	The communal council takes action to promote the development of the gender aspect	• Number (proportion) of actions favouring women and minority or excluded groups within the AIP
	The commune associates the minority groups and the excluded groups with decision-making	• Percentage of young people, women or minority groups having participated in the IAP assessment

ANNEX 2: PROCEDURE FOR USING THE PUBLIC FINANCES CIRCUIT FOR THE LDF OF BENIN

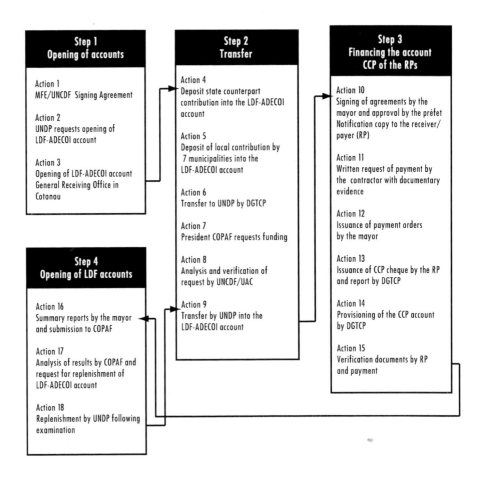

Step 1
Opening of accounts

Action 1
MFE/UNCDF Signing Agreement

Action 2
UNDP requests opening of
LDF-ADECOI account

Action 3
Opening of LDF-ADECOI account
General Receiving Office in
Cotonou

Step 2
Transfer

Action 4
Deposit state counterpart
contribution into the LDF-ADECOI
account

Action 5
Deposit of local contribution by
7 municipalities into the
LDF-ADECOI account

Action 6
Transfer to UNDP by DGTCP

Action 7
President COPAF requests funding

Action 8
Analysis and verification of
request by UNCDF/UAC

Action 9
Transfer by UNDP into the
LDF-ADECOI account

Step 3
Financing the account
CCP of the RPs

Action 10
Signing of agreements by the
mayor and approval by the préfet
Notification copy to the receiver/
payer (RP)

Action 11
Written request of payment by
the contractor with documentary
evidence

Action 12
Issuance of payment orders
by the mayor

Action 13
Issuance of CCP cheque by the RP
and report by DGTCP

Action 14
Provisioning of the CCP account
by DGTCP

Action 15
Verification documents by RP
and payment

Step 4
Opening of LDF accounts

Action 16
Summary reports by the mayor
and submission to COPAF

Action 17
Analysis of results by COPAF and
request for replenishment of
LDF-ADECOI account

Action 18
Replenishment by UNDP following
examination

Source: ADECOI (2004) MPO, Benin

Note:

CCP: Postal deposit account

MPO: *Manuel de procédures et d'opération* (Operational manual)

UAC: *Unité d'appui conseil* (Advice Unit)